# YOUR DREAMS

## ARE TOO SMALL

By Joe Tye

This is a work of fiction. Any resemblance to any real person living or dead (other than perhaps the author himself) is strictly a coincidence.

Published by: Paradox 21 Press

Book Design & Illustration: Studio 6 Sense • www.6sense.net

ISBN#: 9781-887511-28-5

1. Motivation 2. Success 3. Achievement 4. Goals

# UNSOLICITED COMMENTS FROM READERS OF THE FIRST EDITION

*Your Dreams Are Too Small* is one of the best books I've *ever* read. This book absolutely blew me away for the entire read. In my opinion, it ranks right up there with the classics… What Tye has done in this book is provide us a roadmap to achieving our own goals and dreams by encasing his wisdom within a really fun and inspiring story. I would – and will – recommend this book to anyone."

—Bob Burg, author of *Endless Referrals* and *The Go-Giver*

"This is a note to say how much I have enjoyed reading your book, *Your Dreams Are Too Small.* It is a small but powerful life-changing book that will help anyone who is on the journey to becoming a better person. It is easy to read and very entertaining. I have taken the liberty of recommending it to many of my Mary Kay independent consultants and Director friends. I foresee this being a mainstay of my personal library and one that will make a perfect gift. It would benefit any library and I highly recommend it."

—Diane Pascoe

"Just reading *Your Dreams Are Too Small* has been a transforming experience for me. Implementing and sharing what I have learned is going to be even better!"

—Angie Foster

"Thank you so much for writing such an amazing book, *Your Dreams Are Too Small.* I am a well read person, and I travel for a significant part of my job!! Every opportunity I get I sell that book to everyone I meet. We need more of those books!!!!"

—Kelli Trudel

"This book reminded me why I started my company, the dreams I had and the challenges I endured, it reminded me of the goals that I have yet to realize and the fact that even with these recent events, I should not be deterred."

—A struggling entrepreneur

# Other books by Joe Tye

*Never Fear, Never Quit: A Story of Courage and Perseverance*

*Staying on Top When the World's Upside Down*

*Personal Best*

*The Winning the War with Yourself Field Manual*

*Leadership Lessons from The Hobbit and The Lord of the Rings*

*The Farmer*

*Take the Stairs* (With Roger Looyenga)

*The Healing Tree: A Mermaid, A Poet, and A Miracle*

*The Twelve Core Action Values*

*The Florence Prescription: From Accountability to Ownership*
(with Dick Schwab)

*All Hands on Deck: Building a Culture of Ownership*
(due in July 2010)

*Pray for Your Friends: The 8 Prayers of Job*
(due in December 2010)

# DEDICATION

For Sally, Annie, and Doug

If no other dream ever came true,
the love of my family would be enough

# CONTENTS

# Introduction

A lot has happened in the ten years since the first edition of *Your Dreams Are Too Small* was published. We've experienced terrorist attacks, stock market crashes, economic recessions, mass layoffs, and a great depression of the emotional variety. Unfortunately, these challenges have not yet been sufficiently serious to yank us out of the culture of mindless self-indulgence and entitlement that is a plague on the Western world. They have not sparked us to dream bigger dreams, and to commit ourselves to the realization of those dreams, whatever the cost. At least not yet.

If anything, the principles outlined in *Your Dreams Are Too Small* are more relevant today than they were in 2000. And if anything, the opportunities are more plentiful and magnificent. For example, the Internet has completely changed the rules of the game in business. Whether you are opening a new restaurant, starting a consulting firm, writing a book, or getting into a direct sales and marketing business, the playing field has been leveled. Today, anyone can set up a website, start an e-mail newsletter, and use social media to create a worldwide community of followers and customers.

Something that hasn't changed is the imperative to dream big dreams, to have the courage to take action to make those dreams real, and the determination to persevere in the face of every difficulty. For most of us, despite this wealth of opportunity, our dreams are still too small. But as Charlie McKeever discovered in Your *Dreams Are Too Small*, and as you will discover as you read the book and apply the principles in your own life, when you take immediate and sustained action in pursuit of your dreams, they become memories of the future.

As I was working on this new edition, I had an incredible revelation. Although I didn't realize it at the time, when I first wrote this book in 1999, I was writing an autobiography in advance. Though the details are different, on a broad canvas my goals and dreams for Values Coach Inc. closely parallel the goals and dreams Charlie McKeever had for The Courage Place. And my journey over the past decade has followed some of the same twists and turns that I originally created for Charlie in this story, thinking that I was writing fiction.

Dream a big dream, make it a memory of the future, and expect a miracle. *Your Dreams Are Too Small* is a fictional story, but it's also true. I hope you will enjoy the story, but more important I hope that it will serve to galvanize your own big dreams, and inspire you to transform them into your memories of the future.

CHAPTER ONE

# See the World As It Really Is, Not As It Used to Be, As You Wish It Were, Or As You Fear It Might Be

Charlie McKeever had sensed that things were going downhill for some time. It began when he noticed a faint wisp of apprehension hanging over his head on the way to work last week. At the time it seemed harmless enough, a benign little cloud that would soon blow over. But in the succeeding days it grew bigger and darker, until this morning he woke up with a dark thunderhead of dread blocking out what on most days was a blue sky brightly illuminated with enthusiasm and optimism. "Today the storm will come," the cloud seemed to promise.

He'd started with Logistics Plus as a junior analyst right out of college, forsaking the MBA route taken by most of the other kids he'd become friends with through St. Johns' Entrepreneurship Club. "LPI is the hottest consulting company in the country today," the campus recruiter boasted. "We're growing fast, and the demand for the type of management consulting we do will keep on growing as technology gets more complex and competition more intense." Charlie had liked the recruiter immediately: bright and enthusiastic, and barely out of school himself.

"The opportunities for advancement are limited only by your energy and initiative. Who knows, you could become the youngest partner in the history of this firm – you've certainly got the intelligence and the work ethic. It's really the perfect job: the excitement of entrepreneurship plus the security of working for an established firm."

Charlie had worked hard for the past 14 years, and had been well-rewarded for his efforts. He and Pam bought a nice house in the suburbs, and their children attended an exclusive private school. But he never did make partner. Each year, there was a different reason – no vacancies, the firm was having a tough year, and finally the fact that he lacked an MBA degree – but the disappointment was always eased with a healthy pay raise and the promise that he would be at the top of the list for consideration next year.

Except this time. When his annual performance appraisal was completed three months ago he was, as usual, praised for his hard work and dedication. "But we really need you to raise the bar, Charlie," Dick Dierdron, the new managing partner, told him. "When I took this office last year, I made it pretty clear that I expected everyone to produce new business. You just haven't stepped up to the plate. You haven't brought any new clients into the firm, nor have you extended the contracts of current clients."

"It's no secret the competition is heating up, and that we've lost some important business to the Lipton Group." He scowled as he spit out the name of LPI's toughest competitor. "Profits are not what they should be. The partners," and he said this as though speaking of some outside body over which he had no influence, "have told me that we'll have to make cutbacks if the situation is not remedied, and remedied very quickly."

Dierdron leaned back in his high-backed leather chair and thumbed through Charlie's personnel file, which had been the only thing resting on top of his perfectly-polished desktop. "You're one of our best consultants, Charlie. We can't afford to lose you, and the partners know it. I personally don't want to lose you, because you're good, and because you're the best teacher we have for new kids coming into the firm." Dierdron adjusted his gold cufflinks in the way he always did to signify that a meeting was almost over.

"But you've got to bring in business, Charlie. Don't just sit here in the office waiting for someone else to bring it to you."

Dierdron dropped Charlie's folder on the desk and was about to stand up when Charlie blurted out, "When am I supposed to be finding all this new business, Dick? I'm working about eighty hours a week now, and you've just charged me with installing the new computer system." In fourteen years, Charlie had never lost his temper, not even raised his voice – especially not at a partner, let alone the managing partner – but suddenly it seemed like a mental dam was stretching to the breaking point, about to release a flood of emotions that Charlie didn't even realize was up there. "I'm in here before the night shift guard leaves every morning and I'm still here when the janitor locks up every night, including Saturday. I've given my life – for cryin' out loud Dick, I hardly know my own kids! Other parents talk about coaching their kids' soccer teams. I don't even have time to see my kids' soccer team play!"

Now Charlie was leaning across the desk, jamming his finger into the fat manila folder that chronicled the history of his working life for the past fourteen years. "Just when do you want me making cold calls, Dick? Between the hours of midnight and six a.m. when I'm not working on projects? Or do you want me to stop running up billable hours during my waking hours?"

As Charlie's emotions flared, he felt the old familiar pop of a mental circuit breaker somewhere up there, shutting down his anger and causing him to take a deep breath and sag back into his chair. "I'm sorry, Dick, but I just can't do it all. I don't know what you expect of me. I'm working as hard as I possibly can, and even now I can't keep up. But if you want new business, you know me, I'll do the best I can to bring in new business."

Dierdron scribbled something onto a sheet of paper and passed it across the desk. "That's your raise for this year, Charlie. With everything so tight, we're not doing very much for anyone." Charlie picked up the paper and stuffed it into his shirt pocket without looking at it, and stood to go. Dierdron rose as well, then walked around to the side of the desk and propped one leg on the corner so as to be half standing, half sitting. "Charlie," he said, and though his expression seemed to have mellowed slightly, his voice retained its stern edge, "I want you to be clear about one thing." Charlie had stopped by the door and now stood with one hand on the knob, the other in his pocket. "What's that, Dick?"

"You're working these crazy hours because you choose to, and for no other reason." Dierdron let the accusation hang in the air for a moment until, uncomfortable in the silence, Charlie retorted, "What do you mean, because I choose to? The work must be done."

"Of course the work must be done, and of course you will be held accountable for getting it done. But that doesn't mean you have to do it all by yourself. After fourteen years, you're still doing a lot of the same kind of thing you did as a brand new junior analyst, and you haven't grown into the work we expect of an experienced associate – like growing new business. You've got to learn how to delegate more, to ask for help more, so that in turn I can delegate more important work to you."

This was the first time in his entire tenure with LPI that Charlie had been directly criticized, and he didn't like it. It wasn't the LPI way to stick someone's nose in their faults, and he could feel the hair rising on the back of his neck.

As if reading his mind, Dierdron cut off Charlie's train of thought. "It's Thursday afternoon, Charlie. Why don't you go find one of the new analysts to pick up for you. Take a long weekend away from the office. Go off by yourself somewhere and think about it. Are you going to grow with us or not? You're at a fork in the road, Charlie. It's time to make a decision, time to commit."

Dierdron walked back to his desk, picked up the phone and punched in a number. "Hey Ben, it's Dick. I need to talk to you about that Consolidated Banking deal. Is this a good time?"

The performance appraisal was over.

Charlie went home early that day, but was back in the office on Friday, being careful to avoid being seen by Dick Dierdron. He only worked half a day on Saturday, and surprised his son by showing up at his soccer game that afternoon.

Things fell back into a routine over the next few months. Charlie brought several junior analysts in on the big computer project with him, made a few cold calls, even bagged a three month extension on the consulting contract with National Warehouse Systems Corp.

He'd almost forgotten about the performance appraisal as he burrowed himself back into his work. But lately bad dreams at night, a periodic sensation of breathless anxiety during the day, and that gathering cloud of dread hanging overhead contributed to a premonition of pain to come. Soon.

It finally did come at 3:30 on Friday afternoon. Dierdron was not one to make small talk. "The partners have decided that we must make reductions in force, Charlie, and your position has been eliminated, effective now. As you know, your contract included a generous severance provision. When you leave my office, Marcella will give you your final paycheck. The partners have all asked me to convey to you their deepest appreciation for your dedicated service, and sincere wishes for a successful future. And on a personal note, I want you to know that if there's anything I can do to be of assistance, you only need to call."

Dierdron came out from behind his desk and extended his right hand. "Charlie, now that you are no longer an employee here, I can tell you something I've believed for a long time, but simply could not say." When Charlie refused to take Dierdron's hand, rather than turning away his former boss stepped closer and put a hand on Charlie's shoulder, looking him square in the eye.

"Wake up, Charlie. You don't belong up here, hidden away in a cubicle with your nose buried in computer printouts. You're just too smart, too talented. Why don't you use all that talent to build something for you, not for someone else?" Dierdron's eyes bore in, and Charlie looked at the floor.

"You're not an analyst, Charlie, you're not a consultant. People like you can make big things happen. People like you change the world. You've got more potential than me and all the other partners here wrapped up together. What are you waiting for?"

Charlie broke away and turned the doorknob. For the last time he looked at the photo of Mt. Everest that was on the wall opposite of Dierdron's desk, with the inscription that read "Big Hills Are The Only Ones Worth Climbing."

"I know you're pretty upset right now, Charlie, but I hope you'll think about it. That's where you belong, up there on top of the mountain, not down below as part of the support team. You've got the brains and the energy and the work ethic, Charlie. You just don't have the dream. Why don't you use this opportunity to look for your dream. Who knows, you might find the real Charlie McKeever buried under all of those duties and obligations you don't have to shoulder again for a while."

Charlie looked from the mountain back down to the door handle, hesitated for a moment, then twisted it slowly.

"I'm really sorry, Charlie. I meant it when I said I'll help in any way if you just..."

Charlie stepped out of the office and pulled the door shut behind him, cutting off the tail end of Dierdron's last sentence.

Charlie sat on the deck of The Patio, a favorite after-work hang-out of the executive and professional crowd, looking out over the bay. The sun was high and a soft breeze was blowing across the bay, momentarily transporting Charlie back to the family vacation in Belize several years ago. He was tempted to just let go, to drift with this moment. This was the first time he'd really ventured forth from his house since being fired two weeks earlier, and the first time in many years that he'd sat in the sun on a weekday (a workday!) with nothing more important to do than sit in the sun.

But Cheryl von Noyes would be arriving at any moment, so he had to remind himself to not look too chipper. Cheryl, an old friend from the Entrepreneurship Club at St. Johns, had recently lost her job as controller of a local manufacturing company. Charlie knew she'd received only a meager severance and suspected she'd be pretty desperate, so he didn't want to make her feel bad by being too happy or upbeat himself. He slumped down into the chair, put his cheeks into his hands, and looked out over the water, conjuring up mental images of Dick Dierdron giving him the axe.

"Hey, Charlie McKeever!" Cheryl had slipped up to the table while Charlie was working to resurrect his anger. "You don't look very happy for a man who's just been liberated after fourteen years of hard labor!" Cheryl plopped joyously down into the chair beside Charlie and leaned over to wrap him in a bear hug. Over his shoulder, he could see how interesting he had become to everyone else on the deck, now that they thought he was a newly liberated ex-con.

"My word, Cheryl," Charlie exclaimed, trying to keep his balance as his chair tipped toward his friend, "you sure are happy for someone who's just gotten canned!"

"Are you kidding," Cheryl laughed, "I wasn't canned, I was let out of the can! And with every new day of freedom, I appreciate all the more how big a favor they did for me."

The couple at the next table picked up their drinks and moved inside. Evidently, the thought of sitting adjacent to two people just out of "the can" was too much for them.

'So how are you doing, Charlie Swordfish?" That was his name in the computer stock market game they used to play, and she still used it.

Charlie sighed and looked at his feet, now sporting Velcro-laced sandals instead of the polished black wingtips he'd worn nearly every day for the past fourteen years. "Oh, well, I guess..." Charlie sighed again and looked at a point far beyond the horizon. "I guess I'm doing as well as any unemployed bum could be doing, after his life's work and his future dreams have been ripped away from him." The phrase sounded every bit as eloquent as he'd hoped it would be when he'd rehearsed it earlier that day. "I'm looking around, but it's pretty hard when you've got the Scarlet "F" – Fired! – as the last line on your resume."

Charlie sighed again, and glanced to see if he'd hit a sympathetic vein. Instead, Cheryl was laughing.

"Oh, Charlie! You always did know how to crack me up!" Charlie started to smile with her, and soon was laughing himself, overlooking his annoyance that she was laughing at *him*, at his carefully prepared little speech. "What's so funny, Cheryl von Nosey?" That had been her *nom de guerre* for the computer game.

She hardly looked any older, Charlie thought. Her hair was now cut short in the layered pixie style that so many women executives seemed to be wearing these days. She was wearing a white shirt with a silk scarf and a red blazer, prompting Charlie to wonder if she had a job interview scheduled later that afternoon. On the blazer's lapel was a large gold pin forming the letters "FPN" in bold block letters. There was a small jewel at one end, with indentations evidently marking the planned homes of more in the future.

"Sorry, but as you were talking I had this picture pop into my mind of you and your family sitting under a bridge, warming your hands over a trashcan fire." Cheryl laughed again at the image. "Can you imagine anything more ridiculous, especially for the guy voted most likely to win big by the Entrepreneurship Club?"

"Well, yeah, as a matter of fact I can," Charlie sniffed. "You must obviously have a new job already lined up to be taking this so lightly."

"Well," she smiled, "yes and no." Charlie hated that answer – it was how the accountants usually responded when he asked if one of his projects was making money. "But I take it from your sad face that you're still looking. How's it going?"

This was not at all what Charlie had envisioned for this meeting. Not only was Cheryl not a broken woman, she was positively ebullient. Instead of raising her up from the depths, he now saw the very real likelihood that he was going to bring her down. He wanted to say something, but was afraid he might cry instead if he tried. Charlie choked a sigh, and as Cheryl's face grew suddenly serious he looked back out at the bay, wishing he were anywhere else in the world but here with this old friend, whose equanimity in facing a catastrophe that had left him an emotional invalid made him feel acutely inadequate.

"Since you asked first, Charlie, I'll tell you. I'm not looking for a job. I am determined that never again will I look for a job, never again place my future in the hands of someone whose only interest is how much money my work puts into their pocket, and whose interest dies the minute creating a more prosperous future for me becomes economically inconvenient for them."

There was no rancor in Cheryl's voice, but her words were wrapped around a steel reinforcing beam. "You know what the letters J-O-B stand for, Charlie? 'Jilted, Obsolete, and Broke!' Why, the word itself comes from the Old Testament – you know, Job, the character who had everything taken away from him? That can happen to anyone who's got a J-O-B."

"But Cheryl," Charlie protested, "not everyone's cut out for entrepreneurship. It can be a big risk."

"I'm not talking about entrepreneurship, Charlie," she replied. "I'm talking about getting back to what's really important: to having work that makes a difference, work that has meaning beyond just making a paycheck. Work you can be passionate about, work you love to do and can do with love. Work that..."

Cheryl was bouncing slightly, and starting to trip over her tongue in her hurried excitement. "Work that can be love made visible. That's what Kahlil Gibran wrote in *The Prophet* – work is love made visible. Wait, listen to this..." Cheryl pulled a small book from her purse and turned to a paperclipped page. "Let me read you a little poem that changed my attitude about work forever." Charlie read the book's cover, unadorned except for a title of apparently hand-calligraphered letters reading *Little Nuggets of Wisdom by McZen.* Cheryl read aloud:

*Someone with a job*
*is never secure;*
*Someone with a calling*
*is never unemployed.*

"It's true, Charlie. If you only have a job, you'll never be secure, no matter how much money you make. If your work is a calling, there'll always be important work to be done, even if the pay is occasionally low."

Charlie shook his head and snorted, "The only calling I want to hear right now is a headhunter calling to tell me about a great high-paying job."

"So you can once again wind up jilted, obsolete, and broke?" Cheryl actually looked angry. "Life's too short to trade it away for money, and if you don't love your work like it's a calling, all the money in the world won't bring you peace."

"I don't know," Charlie replied. "I wouldn't even mind losing a job if I got one of those top-tier golden parachute packages. I could get used to being insecure if I had a bank vault loaded to the brim."

"Don't bank on it," Cheryl retorted. "You remember reading about Mad Dog Dunleavy, the so-called turnaround artist who would come into a company and hack away thousands of jobs to pump up short-term profits – and the stock price – then walk away with a multi-million dollar bonus before the empty shell collapsed behind him?"

"Yeah, sure," Charlie replied. "Only he didn't get away fast enough at the Top Drawer company – the shell collapsed on top of him and he got fired."

"My point exactly," crowed Cheryl. "No matter how high up, someone with a job is never secure."

"No," Charlie shot back "*my* point exactly. "Mad Dog was a dismal failure, but you know as well as I do that his lawyers will squeeze millions out of the Top Drawer board to make him go away. I could live for a long time with that kind of insecurity!"

Cheryl leaned back in her chair and looked at Charlie as if with fresh eyes, and Charlie sensed that she might not like what she was seeing. "Mad Dog is exactly what is wrong with our country today. The man had no values, no guiding vision, no central principles beyond padding his bank account. He didn't care about the people whose lives he affected – whose careers he trashed! He didn't care about whether his company's products made a difference in other people's lives. All he cared about was fattening up an obscene bank account that he built on the backs of the people whose livelihoods he shattered in the name of boosting quarterly profits."

"Why, Cheryl," Charlie said somewhat defensively, "if I didn't know any better I'd say you're becoming a socialist."

"Quite the contrary, Charlie. In fact, I think what Mad Dog and people like him are doing is the opposite of capitalism, and of entrepreneurship. Capitalists and entrepreneurs create value; mad dogs destroy it. Someone like Mad Dog Dunleavy doesn't belong in the same breath with Bill Hewlett and Dave Packard, with Herb Kelleher or Mary Kay Ash, and the others we studied in school. You wanna know what the difference is, Charlie? Those people, those heroes of American capitalism, had a dream, a big dream, a dream that involved creating jobs and growing people, not destroying jobs and humiliating people."

Cheryl realized that in her excitement she was preaching to everyone on the patio, and as she sat back in her chair smiled to think that they must not know what to make of this "ex-con" who so passionately defended the art of capitalistic entrepreneurship. "Charlie, I just can't see you, of all people, wanting to be anything like Mad Dog Dunleavy. In school, we all wanted to be like you – Charlie the Swordfish, Charlie the Swashbuckler, Charlie the man of mountain-sized dreams."

Charlie sipped his Coke. "It's not so easy, Cheryl, when the kids come along, and the mortgage payments and the car payments, and pretty soon the college tuition payments. I guess if I had a bank account the size of Mad Dog's, I'd be a little more adventurous."

"You think Mad Dog's happy? You think he's secure?" Before Charlie even had time to think about answering, Cheryl went on. "Let me tell you, the other day I was going in for an appointment with my shrink and..." Cheryl noticed Charlie's shock at the confession and interjected, "Yeah, I have problems that I can't figure out on my own, and I've learned that being ashamed to ask for help when you need it is a sign of weakness, not strength." Then she continued, "So guess who was in the waiting room when I came out? Go on Charlie, give it a shot – who was sitting there, looking miserable as a starving hound in a rainstorm? That's right Charlie, the Mad Dog himself."

Charlie stared quietly into the depths of his Coke, looking to Cheryl like a poor beaten dog himself. "Sorry I got so carried away, Charlie. I just hate to see you wasting your time, your life, chasing this phantom of security. You can't get it from a job, you can't get it from money. It's got to be from something bigger. You have to have a mission, a vision, a calling."

> **You can't get security from a job, you can't get it from money. It's got to be from something bigger. You have to have a mission, a vision, a calling.**

"What does he do for you?" asked Charlie, still not looking up from his Coke.

"What does who do?"

"Your, uhm, your shrink?"

"Dr. Connors? He helps me see things the way they really are. It's the ultimate challenge in life, you know? To see things as they really are, not as they used to be; not as you wish they were or think they ought to be; not as you're afraid they are or might become; but just simply as they are."

Charlie looked at her, not quite comprehending.

"You just lost a job that, truth be told, you really didn't like and certainly wouldn't have been doing except for the money. Was that a good thing or a bad thing?"

Charlie shrugged, still not in sync with her.

"The answer is yes, Charlie. The answer is yes. That's what Dr. Connors helps me figure out. The world is what it is; part of becoming a real adult is to see the world as it is and for what it is, without having that perception distorted by the lens of your ego, your emotions, your ambition. And to accept it as it is, without judging good or bad, because that's the first step to being able to change it. To understand that Shakespeare was right when he said that something is made good or bad only by the way we think about it."

"Is he nice?"

"What?

"This Dr. Connors, is he... I mean... What I am really trying to ask, Cheryl, is if you have his phone number in case I want to call him."

Cheryl smiled, warmed by a flood of affection for the wounded "swordfish" in front of her. Though he probably never even knew it, she thought, it was his very weakness and vulnerability, his willingness to ask for help, that made him the natural leader of the Entrepreneurship Club. She lifted her purse, extracted one of her business cards, and wrote Dr. Connor's name and number across the top.

"FPN," Charlie commented, trying to be nonchalant as he scanned the card, but already nervous at the prospect of making an appointment to see a psychiatrist, "I noticed that on your pin, as well. What does it stand for?"

"Future Perfect Now," Cheryl replied. "It's my new business."

"Future... Perfect... Now?" Charlie asked. "What is it, what do you do?"

Cheryl pulled another book from her purse, this one bigger than the little book of poetry. "This, Charlie, is my *Dreamcyclopedia*. It contains photographs, news clippings, and other records of my future." She said it with a straight face, so Charlie was reluctant to laugh, but he did smile when he asked, "Your future? Have you discussed this, ahh, dream book with your shrink?"

"Yes Charlie, actually I have. We're working on it together. Rather than trying to take me back through everything that was wrong about my past, he wants me to move ahead and think about everything that's right about my future."

Charlie looked at Cheryl, then at her *Dreamcyclopedia*, then back at Cheryl, searching for some hint that he was about to be socked with a punch line. When it didn't come, he asked, "Well, it sounds, umm, interesting. Will you tell me more about it?"

"Not now Charlie. You're not ready." Cheryl put the book back in her purse and stood up to leave. "Frankly, Charlie, it's not something you'd be interested in right now. Your dreams are too small. As long as your primary fixation is on money and the vain hope for security, FPN has nothing to offer you. Doctor Connors works a lot with a lot of displaced executives. See if he can help you figure things out. Then maybe we can talk again."

She gave Charlie a quick hug and turned to go. "Thanks for the Coke." With a wink toward the eavesdropping neighbors at the next table, she was gone.

***

Midway through the third appointment, Dr. Connors walked over to the picture window and looked down. It had never occurred to Charlie to wonder what was on the other side of that window, engrossed as he had been in telling Dr. Connors his story, and answering his periodic questions. He was beginning to wonder what Cheryl saw in the man, since so far Charlie had done almost all the talking.

"Come on over," the doctor said in a tone that was more directing than asking, "take a look at this."

Charlie looked down into the courtyard below, in the middle of which was a swimming pool shimmering in the sun. "It's the therapy pool for PT patients," the doctor explained, adding with a sly smile that on particularly hot days other inhabitants of the complex were known to take a dip. "Think of that pool as your subconscious mind, Charlie. It's the real you, the authentic you, a 'you' that has total clarity, perfect serenity, and that is connected with infinite wisdom and knowledge of all things."

Charlie looked into the pool, trying to imagine himself in that form, peaceful and all-knowing. The surface was so calm he could read the lane marker numbers on the bottom as clearly as if there had been no water in the pool at all.

"Uh-oh," said Dr. Connors, "here comes the little troublemaker that has deceived you into thinking that he's the real you." He pointed down to the walkway that linked the swimming pool with the entrance of the physical therapy unit, where an adult therapist was futilely trying to restrain a young boy in a bathing suit who, despite a noticeable limp, was surging toward the pool.

"What do you mean, the little trouble..."

"Shh!" Dr. Connors held up a finger to his mouth. "Watch what happens to the letters at the bottom of the pool." Just then, the little boy leaped into the pool with a lopsided cannonball, his splash forcing the therapist to make a quick retreat from the pool's edge. He came up laughing, arms flailing, and splashing water in the direction of the therapist now standing a safe distance away.

"Read the words embedded in the tile at the deep end of the pool." Dr. Connors instructed. "What do they say?"

"You're kidding, right?" The surface of the pool was now so furiously rippled that Charlie couldn't even see the bottom, much less make out any words that might be printed there.

"Sit down, Charlie." Rather than going back to his chair, Dr. Connors perched himself atop the desk as Charlie took his place back on the sofa against the wall. "Now, close your eyes and just relax. Let the image of the pool, before it was disrupted by that little boy, come gently back into your mind. And just to help you hold away the disrupting influence of the little troublemaker for a moment, I'm going to recite some words that are probably very familiar to you. 'The Lord is my shepherd, I shall not...'"

"Goodness and mercy!" Charlie blurted out. "Those are the words in the pool! Goodness and mercy. I saw them in my mind as clear as day, as soon as I knew you were reciting the Twenty-Third Psalm!"

Dr. Connors smiled. "When I was in med school, someone had posted a sign on our locker room bulletin board that asked 'what is it you know but are pretending to not know?' Tell me, Charlie, what did you know fourteen years ago when you were involved in the Entrepreneurship Club that you are pretending to not know today?"

Charlie closed his eyes again, let his thinking drift back to the classroom where they met every Thursday evening to share their big dreams. As clearly as he'd seen the letters on the bottom of the pool, Charlie now saw the faces of his fellow students riveted as he described his dream of building a worldwide organization of people who were not only committed to making the world a better place, but who received economic rewards commensurate with their individual contribution toward that goal. "My God," Charlie thought, "look at them. They actually took me seriously! They thought I was really going to make it happen."

From a deep recess of his mind, Charlie thought he heard his mother's voice yelling out: "Not yet Charlie! Don't you go in that water until I can come and watch you." Then he heard the slapping of bare feet and a boy's voice – his own voice as a little boy – shrieking. "The pool! Last one in's a rotten egg!" He could hear the feet slapping against the pool deck, close now. Then he imagined himself back in the classroom, looking around at the faces of his fellow students. Cheryl was speaking: "And Charlie is so right! The most important thing about what he's saying is..."

**SPLASH!!**

The image of the classroom erupted into a maelstrom of ripples. "You can't keep me out of the pool," the little boy's voice was shouting, though Charlie wasn't sure whether the youngster was talking to him or to talking back to the voice of his mother. The little boy was splashing everywhere, creating chaos and confusion. The earlier clarity of his thoughts dissipated into a confused kaleidoscope of images, complete with a soundtrack of criticism, disappointment and pity – all directed at him.

"What did you see, Charlie?"

Charlie opened his eyes, realized he was crying. "I don't know. Cheryl was trying to tell me... it was something really important... but the kid jumped in the pool before she said it and I lost the image." Charlie started crying again, feeling stupid for crying and thankful for the Kleenex on the table next to the sofa.

"Charlie, we're almost at the end of our hour, but I'd like to do something I almost never do. Because it's coming up on noon, my next hour is open. I'd like to help you learn more about that little troublemaker who's playing around in your pool. Can you stay?"

Charlie forced a smile. "I'm unemployed, Doc. I've got no place to go and all the time in the world to get there."

Dr. Connors brought them both a cup of coffee, then pulled the blinds to darken the room. He asked Charlie to close his eyes, relax, and let his mind just drift freely.

When Charlie seemed sufficiently relaxed, Dr. Connors continued. "Now, I am going to describe several situations to you, and you tell me in a sentence or two what you think is going on. Don't worry about trying to get what you think is the right answer, just describe the first scenario that pops into your mind. OK?"

Charlie nodded his assent and Dr. Connors went on. "Number one. You've been called into your boss' office. He's there with the company lawyer, the head of security, a uniformed police officer, and another man you don't recognize. They're all frowning and everyone seems distinctly uncomfortable the moment you step into the room. What's about to happen – first thing that comes to your mind?"

"I'm about to be fired and escorted to my car by the security guard and the cop to make sure I don't cause trouble or steal anything on the way out."

"Alright," said Dr. Connors, "here's the next one. You've applied for a job, one that you really want, and it seems to be going very well. They call to say you are their preferred candidate, but they want to check a few references, including the boss who just fired you. One week later you get a letter regretfully informing you that you were not selected for the job. What happened?"

"That's obvious. The S.O.B. wasn't content with just trashing my job, he had to trash my career as well, so he gave one of those politically correct references that between the lines says that he thinks I'm a loser and that they could do better."

Dr. Connors paused for a moment and Charlie could hear the scratching of his pen before he went on. "Here's number three. It takes you ten months to find another job, but the chemistry just isn't there with the new boss, and very quickly you get fired. The next search takes almost a year, and in your third month on the job the company announces a layoff that wipes out your job. Another two years go by and you still don't have a job in the traditional sense. Describe your circumstances."

Charlie groaned. "Pam and I have moved back in with my parents and I contribute to the household budget by mowing lawns and delivering pizza."

"OK. Next one. Instead of taking a traditional job, you decide to start your own business." Connors noted that Charlie grimaced at that prospect, and went on. "Things come together much more slowly than you had anticipated, and you exhaust every available source of cash – savings, retirement accounts, everything. You're starting to bounce checks and still have no sales on the books. What happens next?"

"Bankruptcy." Charlie spit the word out as if it was an insect that had somehow crawled into his mouth, and when Doctor Connors remained silent, he added, "Bankruptcy, humiliation, divorce; I'm sure you've seen it all, Doc, what comes next? Drugs and alcohol? Suicide?"

"Relax, Charlie. Let me ask the questions for now. You'll have your chance soon enough. Now, for these next three, I want you to put yourself in the state of mind you were in right after you got fired. Try to bring back, as vividly as possible, all the emotions you were feeling, as though it had just happened."

Charlie looked as if he'd been kicked in the stomach. Connors went on. "You're sitting at home going through the want ads when suddenly a memory pops into your head from college days. What is that memory, the first thing you think of?"

"Failing calculus during my freshman year."

"Number two. You're sitting at home going through the want ads and the phone rings. It's a headhunter who tells you that you're one of two final candidates for the job you really want. She says that you know the other candidate, but she can't reveal who it is. Who do you immediately suspect?"

"Jeremy Potts. Lord, I don't have a chance. Even I would offer the job to Potts before I gave it to me."

"One more, Charlie. You get a call from your banker. He tells you that the big conglomerate to which they sold your mortgage has a policy against carrying loans on people who are unemployed. If you don't have a job within six weeks, they're going to demand full and immediate payment of your home loan. You take out a pad of paper and start making a list of all your options. Tell me what's on your list."

Charlie thought for a minute. "All I need is to have a job? Any job?" Eyes still closed, he took Connors' silence to be acquiescence and continued. "Well, I could get a job down at the Stay-Put plant. They're always looking for people to fill the night shift, and really don't care what your qualifications are as long as you can make your arms go up and down in time with the assembly line. I could... let's see. I could go to Pam's dad and ask him to list me as one of his employees, but with the understanding that he didn't have to pay me a salary. I could always go back to delivering pizza like I did in college. Is that enough?"

"That's enough Charlie. Go ahead and open your eyes and let's talk about what you've said. What you just completed is a standardized test. The first series of questions measure where you fall on the optimism-pessimism scale, and the second set measures how you respond to anxiety. Taken together, Charlie, these two tests often show how seriously your conscious mind – if you will, the little troublemaker in the pool – can distort your perception of reality. Actually, there *is* a correct response to each of the questions you just answered. And you missed every single one, Charlie, which suggests to me that your future success and happiness depend on doing some reprogramming up here," and Dr. Connors pointed to his own temple.

"Let's go through them one-by-one," Connors said, returning to his chair. "In the first scenario, when you were called into your boss' office, you automatically assumed you were about to be fired. In fact, the boss' car had been stolen from the parking lot. The person you didn't know was his insurance agent. The only reason you were called was to see if you'd noticed anything unusual, and for the boss to ask you for a ride home."

"Oh come on!" Charlie protested. "That's so unlikely! You can't just..."

"Charlie," Doctor Connors cut him off, "this question measures your tendency to jump to pessimistic conclusions. At least you didn't automatically assume that you were about to be arrested because someone had planted illegal drugs in your desk – you'd be surprised how many people do – but your response is toward the negative end of the scale. It's especially important for you to watch out for this, because over time people tend to find what they're looking for."

"Are you saying that after fourteen years I got fired because I expected to be fired?"

"You tell me, Charlie. Did you expect to be fired? Were there times you imagined it happening? Planned what you would say when it did? In fact, Charlie, were there times that in your imagination getting fired was actually a relief, the lifting of a burden? Were there times when being able to tell the boss what you really thought felt pretty good?"

"Guilty on all counts." Charlie smiled sheepishly.

"The second scenario, the one where your boss was asked for a reference? Here's what actually happened. The hiring company hit hard times and imposed an across-the-board hiring freeze. But rather than tell you that, it was easier to just send the standard rejection letter. Your boss actually gave you a very nice recommendation."

Charlie looked skeptical.

"Remember what you told me his last words were as you were walking out? Something about wanting to help? Do you think he was lying to you? Laying a trap so he could deliberately wreck your opportunity to make a living?"

"Well, when you put it that way."

"It's another of the problematic behaviors of the little troublemaker in the pool. Needing to have someone to blame when things go wrong, rather than accepting that sometimes things simply go wrong. He ends up creating villains where there are none. But if you react as though there are villains out there, you invariably create enemies – in your own mind first, and then in the real world as you respond to situations in inappropriate ways."

Charlie shifted uncomfortably, recalling the satisfaction he'd felt at closing the door on Dierdron's parting offer to help. It was sincerely meant, Charlie knew in his heart. Dierdron would have given a reference so glowing it would have embarrassed him to hear it. And if that's true, Charlie thought, then maybe he was also telling the truth when he said I had more potential than to spend the rest of my career at LPI. Instead of being a villain, maybe he actually believed he was doing me a favor by pushing me out the door.

"In the third scenario, where you lost two jobs almost as soon as you got them, your response was that you moved back in with your parents, and took on menial odd jobs. What really happened," and at this Dr. Connors smiled at the paradox of claiming to know more about Charlie's future than he did himself, "is that you went back to Logistics Precision and signed them up as the first customer in what very quickly became a multi-million dollar business called McKeever Enterprises."

Charlie rolled his eyes.

"Wake up, Charlie," Dr. Connors admonished. "Isn't that a more likely scenario than moving back home and delivering pizza?"

Charlie nodded, reluctantly.

"In each question, you were mentally projecting the inevitability of the worst possible outcome. I see it all the time. Someone loses a job, and next thing you know in their own mind their family is starving because they're the only one who can't seem to find another job."

Charlie smiled, even more sheepishly this time. He'd been doing an awful lot of awfulizing lately.

"In scenario number four, where you ran out of money and start bouncing checks, your first response was a declaration of bankruptcy. Actually, Charlie, that's the all-too-common practice of blowing things out of proportion, something else the little troublemaker is good at. In fact, you have significant equity in your home, don't you?"

Charlie nodded, thinking of the frequent letters from his bank and others offering him home equity loans. He could support his family for a long time on what he could borrow in that manner if he had to.

"The next three scenarios measured your response to anxiety." Dr. Connors pulled a form from his desk drawer, stuck it into the clipboard, and scribbled a few notes on it. "Anxiety is the mortal foe of creative thinking and decisive action. A mind that is clouded with anxiety conjures up all sorts of fears, fears that paralyze your initiative. Fear is the most malignant of all emotions. Your own fears can create a prison more confining than any iron bars. Let's see how you did."

**Fear is the most malignant of all emotions. Your own fears can create a prison more confining than any iron bars.**

Connors looked back at his clipboard. "When the mind is full of anxiety, memories of past failures loom very large and seem very likely to be repeated, while past successes seem diminished and in any event unlikely to repeat themselves. When I asked you to put yourself in a state of acute anxiety and then to remember something from your college days, what was your first memory?

"Failing calculus," Charlie responded.

Dr. Connors nodded, and asked, "You have a lot of wonderful memories from college, don't you?" Charlie smiled, seeing a torrent of images flashed by: meeting Pam in the library, the night on the beach when he proposed and she said yes, being elected president of the Entrepreneurship Club, even delivering pizza in his old beat up Honda.

"If, instead of asking you to experience anxiety, I had put you in a frame of mind that was at peace and full of courage and confidence, you would have selected one of those other, more positive memories as your first choice. When you're anxious, the little troublemaker becomes like a rabbit frozen in the headlights of fear. He dredges up memories of past failures and frustrations to frighten you out of taking any risk. The unfortunate paradox is that only by taking some risk will you ever alleviate the root cause of your anxiety.

"The second thing that happens is the anxious mind distorts your perception of current reality. When you're paralyzed by fear, your problems always seem bigger and more intractable than they really are, while your own resources seem to shrink away to insignificance. When I asked who you thought the other candidate was for the job you wanted, you immediately came up with Jeremy Potts. Why was that, Charlie?"

Charlie shrugged.

"Can you think of anyone, anyone at all, who you would less rather be stacked up against in the competition for a job than Jeremy Potts?"

Charlie shook his head. "Nobody. He's the best. At everything he does. He could walk into any job he wanted."

"So why assume Jeremy? Why not Elmer Fudd or Mr. Magoo or Dilbert? Surely you know people who are down at that capacity level, don't you?"

Charlie smiled, broadly this time. "Absolutely. In fact, I used to work with quite a few people like that."

"And what if I told you the job you had applied for was assistant librarian over at the college, rather than being the high-powered executive job I think you probably had in mind. How would Jeremy do in that job?"

"He'd go berserk the first week, with no enemies to conquer and no troops to lead, just books to take care of."

"And what if you got that job, at least as something temporary. How would you do?"

"Actually, John," Charlie used the first name without even thinking about it, the first time he had done so, "I'd love it. Two things I love are good books and being left alone to do my own work, and that job would give me both."

"So any library board that hired Jeremy over you would be making a grievous mistake, right?"

"In that case, yes."

"Between now and the next time we get together, Charlie, why don't you try assuming things in your favor? Assume a field that plays to your strengths and desires, not someone else's, and see if that doesn't give you a different – a bigger and brighter – picture of your own future."

"Which brings me to the third anxiety scenario. When you are under anxiety's fat thumb, you simply close your eyes to opportunities right in front of you which, if you took them, could lead to circumstances that would chase the anxiety away. When you had to have a job or risk losing your home, all you could think of were menial jobs – jobs that would not challenge you, satisfy you, or reward you."

"But you told me I had to have the job right away," Charlie protested.

"Yes, I did. And how long would it have taken for you to go down to Kinko's and have them make up business cards for Charlie McKeever, president of McKeever Enterprises?"

"That wouldn't have worked!"

"Why not? Many of my clients do exactly that. They make up business cards, but have no idea what their business will do until they sign up their first customer. And guess what, Charlie – they usually end up with more money and greater security than the people who think they're opting for money and security by taking jobs they really don't like.

"The hardest job in the world, Charlie, is to see reality as it really is – to not believe the twisted caricature that the little troublemaker wants to paint. You've got to break out of what I call the Iron Triangle of False Personality – Ego, Emotion and Ambition – before you can become the real you, the authentic, meant-to-be you. But that has to wait for another time, because my waiting room's going to start backing up if I don't move along here."

Charlie stood up and extended his right hand. "Thanks, John. This has been more enlightening than you'll ever know. You've really given me some things to think about."

"That's good, Charlie. Let me give you one more – sort of the ultimate paradox that I feel you will soon confront face-to-face. Your success depends upon your ability to first see and accept reality as it really is, but then at the same time to expect the miracle that will be necessary to change that reality into what you want it to be as you create your own future."

"Now there's a thought," exclaimed Charlie. "Creating my own future!"

"I don't think we'll need much longer," Dr. Connors said, patting Charlie on the shoulder as he stepped out of the office.

CHAPTER TWO

# KNOW WHO YOU ARE, WHAT YOU WANT, AND HOW YOU'RE GOING TO GET IT

"What do you do?"

The question was innocent enough. Charlie had answered it thousands of times before: "I'm a senior consultant with Logistics Precision. We're a management consulting firm that helps businesses become more profitable by developing effective competitive strategies." The words were even printed on the back of his business card. Until now, he'd never realized the extent to which he relied upon his business card to double as an identity card.

Charlie and Pam were at a fund-raiser for the local symphony, which had been his wife's favorite cause for many years. So far, he'd been successful at staying off to the side of the room, but now this elegant older woman, wearing more gold than even the most successful dentist would mold in a lifetime, wanted to know, "what do you do?" Charlie kicked himself for not having prepared for the question.

"I'm, well, I'm between jobs right now, "he stammered. "I'm looking at..."

She cut him off with a condescending pat on the side of the arm. "How interesting, dear." She was already looking past Charlie to see who else was in the room. "I'm sure something will come up." And she walked off.

Charlie was mortified. "I'm sure something will come up!" As if he was just sitting around all day, waiting for something to come up! Who did she think she was, anyway, to write him off as being unworthy of conversation simply because he was "between jobs?"

"Well, what did you and Madam Butterfly discuss in your little corner over here?" Pam glided up and took his arm. Short and spunky, she was his counterweight, buoying him up when he was in danger of sinking, and keeping him grounded when he was about to buy a one way ticket on a flight of fancy.

"Madam Butterfly?"

"That was Wanda Wilmington. She's been chair of symphony society for, oh, the past eighty years or so. How much did she get you to pledge?"

"Me? Hah! The minute I told her I was unemployed, she disappeared faster than your father used to when Nathan needed his diaper changed. In fact, the look on her face was very much the same."

Pam held Charlie's arm as she laughed. "Yes, that would be the Madam Butterfly I've come to know and love. Her time is for sale to the highest bidder, or should I say to the highest donor. She can be pretty ruthless, but without her the symphony would have folded years ago."

"How awful!" Charlie moaned, prompting a sharp poke in the ribs.

"How would you know anyway? I could never drag you away from the office long enough to hear them play!"

"Oh, yes you did. And it really was awful!"

"Now that's not fair, to judge the symphony on that one night. Harold was just doing a favor for a Julliard classmate by premiering his first symphony. You should come on a night when they play something beautiful, like Bach, or something bold, like Stravinsky. In fact," she smiled, "they're playing Brahms' second and Beethoven's sixth on Saturday night. Those are two of the cheeriest symphonies ever written, and you can't tell me you've got to be at the office."

Charlie tried to look as though he were making a huge sacrifice. "Well, then, I guess it's a date.".

***

"I felt absolutely stark naked. She asked me what I did, and I couldn't answer. It's like nothing else in my life mattered, only my job description."

Dr. Connors looked across at Charlie and waited for him to say something else. When the silence remained unbroken he asked, "What if, instead of asking you what you do, this Madam Butterfly had asked 'Who are you?' How would you have responded to that question? Who are you, Charlie McKeever?"

Charlie looked toward the window beyond which lay the pool. Though he hadn't noticed it before, he now heard what sounded like a small army of kids splashing in the water. Charlie smiled, realizing that right now it felt as if his little troublemaker had invited an army of friends into his own mental swimming pool. The two sat in silence for a moment.

"Why don't we start with an easier question." Dr. Connors finally broke the silence. "Who are you not?" Charlie didn't respond, so Connors continued. "Let's start with the easiest answer first. You are not your possessions. That sounds so self evident it should go without saying, but the fact is that most people make their first, their most lasting, and frequently their only impression of you on the basis of the clothes you wear, the car you drive, the house you live in, or the country club you belong to. Isn't that what Madam Butterfly did? As soon as she suspected your wallet was empty, you stopped being a real person in her eyes, didn't you? It's pretty disempowering when someone tries to reduce you to the contents of your wallet, isn't it?"

Charlie nodded, but still did not speak. "The second thing you are not, but which other people want to distill you into, is your job.

That's a tougher one to figure out, because even you yourself will often link your identity as a person with what you do for a living. Especially in our culture, occupation and self worth are closely intertwined. That's why the question you recently looked forward to answering is now one you dread, because even in your mind, 'What do you do?' and 'Who are you?' are almost the same question. Am I right?"

**You are not your possessions, you are not your job, you are not what other people think of you.**

Charlie started to nod yes, but his chin seemed to get stuck on the downward swing. He looked at the floor, and was again fighting back tears. At the age of 36, had he become so superficial that his whole identity could be captured on the back of a business card?

"You're at a crossroads, Charlie." Connors looked across the room with an unaccustomed intensity. "You're about to make a decision that could determine the course of the rest of your life." The children had left the pool below, and for the first time in all of his appointments with Connors, Charlie realized that there was a grandfather clock ticking away in the far comer.

"Up to this point in your life, the decisions you've made have primarily been intended to please and impress other people. You tried to do what was expected of you and to be the person you thought they all expected you to be. You've never really stopped to ask the question, 'What should I do to please and impress Charlie,' have you?"

Charlie wasn't even trying to stop the tears now. He shook his head. "No."

"Did you hear about the aborigine who bought a new boomerang?" Dr. Connors laughed softly as he asked the question. Charlie sniffled and shook his head again. "Spent the rest of his life trying to throw the old one away."

Charlie laughed through his tears, then, frantically reached for the Kleenex box on the table next to the sofa.

"That's the question, Charlie. Are you ready to throw away the old boomerang, and to keep throwing it away every time it comes back it you? The old boomerang is caring about what other people think of you; trying to do what you think will please and impress everyone else, even if it makes you unhappy; playing it safe by staying close to the ground when deep in your heart you want to spread your wings and soar, even if at first it's terrifying to fly? Are you ready, Charlie, or do you want to hang on to the old boomerang for a while longer?"

"I think I'm ready," Charlie replied, "but I'm not sure I'd even know where to start. How does one throw away an old boomerang?"

"I won't kid you by saying it's easy, Charlie, but you've already made a critical first step."

"What's that?"

"You recognize that the boomerang is not part of you, that it's something you can throw away and replace, if you want to."

"I want to." Softly, but with conviction.

"Remember last time we were together, when I mentioned The Iron Triangle of False Personality? It's bounded on each corner by ego, emotion, and ambition. Now, each of those things are good, if you manage them effectively by staying outside of the triangle looking in. But most people don't manage them. Instead, they react to ego and emotion, chase false ambitions. They get trapped inside the triangle, and it becomes a prison that prevents their development as a human being, stunts their growth as a spiritual being."

Charlie looked up, a bit surprised. It was the first time Doctor Connors had touched upon a spiritual theme. "Is religion compatible with psychiatry?"

Connors laughed. "Your religion – the church you attend, or don't attend – is your own business. But as long as I'm your counselor, your spiritual life is my business. If your attitude about life is the same as the bumper sticker that used to be popular – 'The one who dies with the most toys wins' – then you're setting yourself up for an incredibly superficial and inevitably painful existence. 'Who are you?' is ultimately a spiritual question, because when you break out of the Iron Triangle of False Personality – Ego, Emotion and Ambition – what you find on the other side is soul."

"The first point of the Iron Triangle is ego. I don't mean ego in the technical sense that Freud described, but rather in the everyday sense you think of when you hear that someone has a big ego, or a fragile ego. It's the embodiment of that troublemaking little kid, whose primary concern is for the opinions of other people. For ego, image is everything, substance is nothing. It was ego that got crushed when Madam Butterfly gave you the brush off. It's ego that still nurses the hurt feelings rather than just letting them go. You've probably heard reference to your inner child? Well, ego can be your inner spoiled brat."

"If ego stands in the way of my discovering soul, then how do I distinguish between the two? Sometimes, it's awfully hard to know just exactly who's talking up there." Charlie crossed his arms and stretched his legs out straight.

"Great question, Charlie, and one I can't answer directly. Let's finish our analysis of The Iron Triangle and see if we can't get a little closer to the answer. Ego is the Great Defender. Its primary purpose is to protect you from being hurt by the outside world, but in doing so it prevents you from touching the world in more positive and constructive ways. It was ego that slammed the door in Dick Dierdron's face when he was offering to help you. It may have felt good at the time, but if nothing else, knowing that someday Dierdron might be an important job reference for you, it was a pretty counterproductive behavior, wasn't it?"

Charlie nodded, but he was starting to get a better appreciation for what Dr. Connors had said earlier. Gaining control of the little troublemaker was the hardest work in the world because it *still* felt good to have closed that door in Dierdron's face, even knowing that he might someday pay a regrettable price.

"When ego wants to get your attention," Doctor Connors began again, "it has a very handy set of chains to yank – your emotions.

Emotions can be a beautiful thing. They make humans unique and special, but all too often they are also the enemy within. The research into emotional intelligence is finally starting to get its due, but not many people who make it as far as my office are aware of it. Ego loves to stir up emotions that make *it* feel good, make *it* feel important, but which can provoke *you* to do things that end up being very self destructive."

Connors went to the sink in his back counter and filled up a big glass of water, which he sat upon his desk. Then he removed a small box from the cupboard above and sat back down. "When ego starts stirring up emotions, it rarely hits on just one. What you often end up with is a confused witches' brew."

Connors tapped the glass. "Crystal clear, like the swimming pool before it was disrupted by our little troublemaker friend. A mind this clear would be a perfect environment for perceiving reality with accuracy and making decisions with clarity, do you agree?"

Charlie nodded his assent.

"When Dick Dierdron fired you, it was excruciatingly painful to your ego, wasn't it?" Charlie nodded again, as the mere thought of that meeting caused his stomach to knot. "So in its agony, your ego started to stir up emotions, didn't it? What were they, Charlie, what were some of the emotions you felt that day?"

Charlie clenched his teeth, feeling like he was being dragged against his will back into a room where he didn't want to be. "Anger," he hissed.

"Ah, good old anger," chortled Doctor Connors as he pulled a small bottle out of the box on his desk and removed the top. "Favorite emotion of Mars, the Greek god of war. Bloody red anger." He squeezed several drops of red food dye into the water. "Nothing better to distort your perception and cloud your thinking than anger." Charlie was momentarily mesmerized by the red dye as it swirled its way through the glass of water, seemingly fighting a losing battle to maintain the integrity of its separate identity.

"What other emotions did you feel that afternoon, other than anger?"

"Fear," Charlie replied without hesitation. "Sheer terror, total panic, heart stopping fear."

"Fear and anger. Never one without the other," Connors said as he squeezed several drops of yellow dye into the water. Charlie watched as the red and yellow, each pretty on its own, melded together into a murky orange. "What else did you feel, as you sat in Dierdron's big office looking across that gigantic desk, knowing that when the meeting ended you would go and he would stay?"

"Envy. At that moment, I think I would have given anything to trade places with him."

"Ah, so let's add a little envy to the brew," Connors said as he squirted green food coloring into the glass, causing the water to become a dark purple. "And what about Dierdron himself, what emotion did you feel toward him?"

"Hate. Pure unadulterated hatred." Charlie shuddered. "It was actually scary to feel that much animosity towards another person, especially one I had considered a friend and a partner just hours before."

Connors squeezed some purple dye into to the concoction on his desk, then stirred it up with his pen. It looked like India ink. Connors picked up the glass and held it out toward Charlie. "Care to drink some of your little brew?"

Charlie recoiled at the thought of putting that vile looking concoction in his mouth.

"This is what happens to your mental clarity when ego starts to stir up all those negative emotions. It goes," and he poured the contents of the glass into the sink, "down the drain."

"So now you're in a mess, aren't you, Charlie? You have a wounded ego stirring up all sorts of painful emotions. How do you deal with that, huh? I'll tell you how: you focus on your ambitions."

Connors was pacing back and forth, more animated than Charlie had ever seen him. "Your fear is painful, so you give yourself an ambition to find another job as quickly as possible to reduce the frightening uncertainty of being unemployed. You hate the little snake – I think that was the word you used to describe Dierdron the last time we met – who fired you, so your ambition wants to think of ways to get back at him."

Charlie squirmed uncomfortably. He had, in fact, been daydreaming about taking critical business away from LPI, and more recently had even begun to sketch out a business plan for doing so.

"Here's the sad fact. None of those ambitions are authentic. They are for things you don't really even want. They are intended to placate ego, and to please and impress other people. Listen, one of my clients has built a very successful career in a profession he despises. He got into it because he thought it would please Mom and Dad, and now he doesn't know how to get out of it, even though Mom and Dad died a long time ago. The rest of the world sees a busy, successful executive with all the luxuries worldly success can buy. But once a week, I see a lost, lonely, disillusioned little man who hates himself and everything he does."

They sat in silence for a long time, now comfortable enough in their relationship that neither felt the need to break into it with unnecessary voice. At last, Connors pulled a book from his shelf and handed it to Charlie. "This is *The Self-Transformation Workbook*, which many of my clients have found to be especially helpful in trying to get a better handle on who they are and what they want."

Charlie took the book and pointed to the Never Fear, Never Quit logo at the top. "I see this on T shirts all over the place. I didn't realize it was more that that."

"I was one of the first members," Dr. Connors smiled. "The movement has come a long way since then."

Charlie started to thumb throughout the workbook, which seemed to be full of ideas, inspirations and exercises. "Your friend Cheryl told me she locked herself into her room with that book and didn't come out until she had worked her way through it, from beginning to end," Connors said. "Judging from what she's done with her life since, I'd say it's made quite an impression."

"You know," Charlie said, "I really need to call Cheryl again. I'm afraid the fragile state of my ego prevented me from really connecting the last time."

"Cheryl has a lot to offer, Charlie. She's going to make a difference in this world."

Connors went back to his shelf and pulled off another book. Charlie recognized it as the *Dreamcyclopedia* that Cheryl had taken from her purse, but this one did not yet have anything in it. "Here's a blank slate, Charlie. Go fill it up with a beautiful future."

***

If anything, today was even more beautiful than the first day Charlie met Cheryl for lunch at dockside on The Patio. Even better, this time Charlie felt the sunshine on the inside as well as on the outside. When she joined him, Charlie noticed that a second jewel now graced one of the indentations in her FPN pin.

"Future Perfect Now," Cheryl was saying, "means just what it says. Instead of waiting around, hoping that a brighter future will somehow happen, we are determined to reach out and grab that future, to start living it now as if it were already a reality, which it actually is, even if it may not have yet showed up on your calendar."

"OK, I believe you Cheryl – you yourself are a living, breathing billboard – but what exactly is FPN? What do you do?"

Cheryl smiled, but shook her head No. "You're not ready yet, Charlie, your dreams are still too small. Until you can let go of them and replace them with big dreams, Mount Everest-sized dreams, it would be worse than a waste of time to tell you about it. You wouldn't get it, you'd blow it off and never come back, and that would really be a shame."

"Well," Charlie replied, "you said that there was something you wanted to walk through with me today. If it's not Future Perfect Now, what is it?"

"This will take most of the afternoon, Charlie, but if you're willing to take the time and work through it with me, it could change your life in a radical, beautiful way, like it has mine. Are you willing?"

"Ready, willing and able... And eager!"

Cheryl unfolded a long sheet of paper with six empty blocks, each progressively smaller, forming a pyramid. "This is the Self-Empowerment Pyramid," she said, writing those words at the top of the page with her heavy black felt tip pen. "It's a powerful tool for figuring out who you are, what you want, and how you're going to get it."

"Starting at the beginning, with IDENTITY at the base of the pyramid," and she wrote that word in big bold letters in the biggest box at the bottom of the page, "we'll use this tool to crystallize your identity, mission, vision, goals, and then the action steps you can start taking right now to make sure that your future is the perfect one you want it to be."

Underneath the word Identity, Cheryl wrote out in longhand "Authenticity," and then the numbers one, two and three. "Crystallizing your identity means to discover the real you, the meant to be you, the authentic you that has probably long been overshadowed by the false you that ego has created to please and impress other people." Charlie could hear echoes of Dr. Connors in Cheryl's voice, but also sensed that she was about to tell him something new and different, and very important.

"There are three steps to cultivating your authentic identity: first, know yourself; second, master yourself; and third, believe in yourself. Since you've spent some time with John Connors, I don't need to tell you about the Iron Triangle of False Personality and how important it is to cut through all the clutter that appears to be part of the authentic you but really just misleads you down the easy road of being what you think other people expect you to be, rather than having the courage and determination to take the more difficult road that leads to being the person you are meant to be."

She checked to see that Charlie was tracking with her then continued, "One of the most simple, practical, and effective methods for defining your true identity is with 'I Am" declarations. I've written one of these for myself at three different levels: spiritual, professional, and personal. Would you like to see them?"

Charlie nodded and she opened her Dreamcyclopedia, which she had placed on the table. She put a piece of paper across the page, so Charlie could only see the top third. "This is my spiritual 'I Am' declaration," she said, then read aloud:

*I am a beloved and beautiful child of God, and have been put on this Earth with an important mission that I alone can fulfill. That mission will be made clear to me as I continue to work and grow, but so long as I am pursuing it with enthusiasm and good faith, I will not be allowed to fail, no matter how severe the obstacles may seem.*

"Whenever someone asks me that universal icebreaking question, 'What do you do?' I tell them about my work with FPN, because that's what they expect to hear. But when I see the covert looks of disapproval, which is fairly often because FPN is pretty far off the beaten path, I remind myself of this 'I Am...' declaration. No matter what someone thinks of my work, they can never take this away from me. It's not a job, it's a life's calling." Cheryl moved the paper down to uncover the second third of the page, and read her professional 'I Am' declaration:

*I am a natural born entrepreneur, and I love nothing better than helping other people grow wealthy and wise right alongside me.*

"There in this one sentence is my entire business philosophy," Cheryl said. "Wealth is not enough without wisdom; my own success is not enough without the success of those around me. I must be creating something of unique and lasting value – the hallmark of an entrepreneur. Whenever I get discouraged – when I've been rejected too often, dejected for too long, and being ejected altogether seems like a real possibility, I center myself on what's most important by mentally declaring who I really am: a natural born entrepreneur with a bone deep commitment to the success of others." Cheryl lifted the paper from the book, revealing the bottom third of the page. Charlie read:

> *I am a loving and compassionate wife and mother, and will do whatever I can to help my family be more harmonious and my children be more successful.*

Cheryl laughed. "Every time I come in the house and see chaos reigning, chores neglected, homework not done, TV blaring and children fighting, I stop, take a deep breath, and before I follow my first instinct I remind myself of who I am and who I want to be. Guess what? Nine times out of ten, what my first instinct would have led me to do was an inappropriate response. It was ego pulling the strings, not soul."

Charlie pointed to the "I Am" declarations. "I know I'm supposed to write my own, but would you mind if I copy yours down. They sort of hit home."

"Not at all," Cheryl replied. "That's how I got started, by massaging someone else's declarations around until they felt right for me."

Behind the number 2 Cheryl wrote the words Master Yourself. "In order to become the authentic you, you need to keep a tight rein on ego, emotions, and ambition. Have you heard about tough love?"

"You mean that 'get tough' philosophy for parents whose kids are into drugs and things like that?" Charlie asked.

"Exactly. Well, your ego is like a truculent little kid who's into drugs of a different type. Drugs like self pity, pessimism, cynicism, and other loser attitudes. And believe me, those negative attitudes and beliefs are just as addictive as narcotics, and just as dangerous. They suck people into a downward spiral that begins with 'learned helplessness' – pretending there's nothing you can do to solve your problems; then swirl downward into the 'blame game' – trying to hold someone other than yourself responsible for those problems;

and culminates in 'victim syndrome' – feeling sorry for yourself because you've somehow been singled out for special abuse. And of course, the spiral never ends, because once you feel like a victim, it just reinforces your belief in your own helplessness and you continue to spiral down into the vortex of despair."

"To become the authentic you, you must be tough with yourself by holding yourself accountable for achieving high standards, values, and performance. By the way, being tough *with* yourself doesn't mean being tough *on* yourself by beating yourself up if you don't live up to those high expectations."

"And third," she continued, writing down the words behind the number 3, "you have to believe in yourself. You have to believe, at the deepest level of your heart, that those I Am declarations are true and authentic. After all, if you don't believe in yourself, who will?"

Cheryl now wrote in big block letters the word MISSION in the second box. "Once you've got a clear fix on who you are, the next step is to crystallize what you're here for. When you go from having a job to having a mission, you become unstoppable. One of the most powerfully motivating and focusing things you can do for yourself is write a mission statement. Have you ever done that, Charlie?"

Charlie shook his head. "No, but every now and then I read the one posted in the lobby at LPI. It sounded pretty much like every other mission statement, and could just as well have applied to a sausage factory as a consulting firm."

Cheryl turned the page on her Dreamcyclopedia and pointed out where she had written her own mission statement:

> *My mission is to help people succeed as entrepreneurs by teaching them how to dream big, think creatively, believe in their own abilities, and act courageously so that they can accomplish magnificent goals.*

"If you dissect my mission statement," Cheryl pointed out, "you'll notice three distinct elements. First is my guiding value, which is magnificence as opposed to mediocrity. That word captures everything I stand for, personally and professionally – raising people's standards and expectations and achieving quantum leaps in their performance and outcomes.

"The second element is the key action that makes my guiding value become real. In my case, it's teaching. Being able to teach other people how to be successful entrepreneurs is more central to my own success than being a successful entrepreneur myself, as paradoxical as that sounds. So when I think of how to spend my limited resources, learning how to be a good teacher is more important than anything else I can do."

Charlie gradually became aware of another presence, and realized that their waitress was standing behind them, looking over his shoulder at Cheryl's dream book. Red faced at being caught eavesdropping, she stammered, "Can I get anything else for you two?" Charlie and Cheryl smiled at each other and the waitress said, "Sorry, I just came over to check on you and got taken in listening. I sure don't want to be a waitress for the rest of my life."

"What are you doing right now to try and get out of that rut, Sarah?" Cheryl asked, reading the woman's name tag.

"Well, it's hard to find much time," Sarah replied. "I'm a single mom, and my boys are at an age where they pretty much need me to be around. But," and at this point Sarah lowered her voice as if she were bringing Cheryl and Charlie into a magnificent conspiracy, "I've been taking this home study course on how to think like an entrepreneur, and it's really opened my eyes to the possibilities out there. It was, like, if I'm still waitressing in five years, it will only be because I made that choice."

Sarah looked uncertainly from Cheryl to Charlie to make sure they really wanted to hear the rest of her story. "One of the assignments my teacher – the guy who does this home study course – gives is to start a new business doing something we've never done before, and to keep at it until we've grossed at least one hundred dollars." When Charlie raised his eyebrows at the token amount, she snapped "It's a lot harder than you think it is!"

"So what are you doing to earn your hundred dollars?" Cheryl asked with genuine interest.

Sarah looked around to make sure she wasn't being observed by her supervisors, then reached into the pocket of her apron and pulled out a large round pin. It was clearly hand-painted, not mass-produced, but just as clearly done by someone with both talent and pride of workmanship. In the middle of the button was painted the head of a bald eagle, which Charlie noticed was actually winking, and around the circumference the words, *Winners Don't Quit!*

"That's my motto," Sarah said proudly. "I'm a winner, and winners don't quit. Working at this job, I have to remind myself of that pretty often."

Charlie caught himself looking at the young woman with new respect. It was funny, he thought, how something as simple as trying to sell little inspirational buttons that she painted in her spare time transformed a generic waitress into a real person with dreams and aspirations. "How much do you sell the pins for?" he asked.

"Well, sir," she replied, almost defiantly, "if price is your most important concern you can get buttons down at Target for about two bucks. If you want a work of art like this that you'll be proud to wear wherever you go, the price is ten dollars." Her eyes never wavered from Charlie's during this entire little speech.

After a brief but awkward silence Cheryl started laughing, between bursts managing to get out the question, "How long did you have to practice that so you could pull that off with a straight face?"

"Lady," Sarah replied, Cheryl's laughter having given her permission to show a softer, more vulnerable side, "you don't even want to know how many hours I stood in front of the bathroom mirror and talked to my kids in their car seats 'til I felt like I could ask for what they're worth. That's one thing the teacher for this home study course really hammers home. You have to rehearse great answers to simple questions like, 'What do you do?' and 'How much does it cost?'"

Charlie extracted a ten dollar bill from his wallet and handed it to Sarah. "After a sales pitch like that, how can I not buy a pin? I'd also like to know where I can sign up for this home study course you mentioned, if you don't mind giving me a phone number or address."

Sarah handed Charlie the pin, then turned to Cheryl. "I've got another one pretty much like it, if you'd like one too."

"Actually, Sarah, I need 150 of them. But I need them for a special function on September 22. Can you make them that fast?"

"At ten dollars a pin?" Sarah asked, looking at Cheryl over the top of her half-moon glasses.

Cheryl smiled and nodded. "You certainly don't need to worry about being a waitress for the rest of your life, Sarah. Ten bucks a pin, but on one condition."

"What condition?"

"This sale doesn't go against your quota. You still have to sell at least ninety dollars worth of pins to someone else to satisfy your homework assignment. Here's my card. Why don't you give me a call next week so we can talk more about what goes on the pin."

Sarah put the card in her pocket. "Thanks a lot. These pins are going to be perfect, you have my guarantee of that. But I'm not ready to stop being a waitress quite yet, so I better get back to work." Sarah turned to go, then looked back at Cheryl. "By the way, I'm already way past my hundred dollar quota. See you next week."

Cheryl started to say something to Charlie, then stopped. "Hey, what happened to your pin?"

"It's in my pocket."

"What's it doing in there? Don't you want people to know you're a winner?"

Charlie rolled his eyes, but did fish out the pin and put it on. "OK, it's on. So where were we, as we dissected your mission statement?"

"Actually," Cheryl said, "Sarah came at just the right time, because she is the third element of my mission statement."

"Excuse me, did I miss something?"

"The first element is my guiding value – magnificence over mediocrity. The second element is my critical action step – teaching skills and attitudes for success. The third element is my intended audience, and that is people who have big dreams and want to achieve them on their own terms. People like Sarah."

"People who want the future to be perfect right now?" Charlie added.

"Precisely. And I predict that I'm going to help Sarah sell a lot more than 150 pins to my friends in FPN, if that's what she really wants to do, but also that she's going to end up doing a lot to help me succeed in my own business." Cheryl smiled. "I knew she had what it takes as soon as I saw her look you right in the eye and tell you that the price was ten bucks, take it or leave it."

Returning to the Empowerment Pyramid, Cheryl now put big block letters in the third box spelling out the word VISION. "What would your world look like if you were being the real you, the authentic you, and pursuing the work that is your true calling? What would be the work you would be doing every day? Where would you be doing it? With whom? Where would you live? In what kind of house? The more clear and detailed the mental map of your perfect future, the more certain you are to take the actions now that will assure it becomes your reality, and probably sooner rather than later."

Cheryl sketched an hourglass on the side of the paper. "This is the way future vision works." She placed her pen on the paper and drew a straight line right across the bottom of the hourglass. "This is the present. My vision of reality is very broad, very accurate. I can tell you precisely about the work I'm doing, the house I live in, anything else you want to know."

Now she drew a second line, parallel to the first but up slightly, closer toward the middle. "This line is tomorrow. I still have a very clear and accurate picture of where I am and what I'm doing, but it's just a bit narrower than it is today, because there's a hint of uncertainty thrown in, isn't there?" Charlie nodded. "Now, if I go out a week or a month," and she drew two more lines, each fractionally shorter and closer to the midpoint, "my vision becomes even more circumscribed, and still more if I go out a year, or two years."

"At some point," and she drew a line straight across the narrow waist of the hourglass, "there is a great deal of uncertainty, because in the intermediate term, so many things are beyond our control. Somewhere out here, maybe three to five years, I really can't tell you with a great deal of confidence and certainty where I will be and what I will be doing."

Cheryl drew a line perpendicular to the horizontal one she'd drawn across the center of the hourglass, then put an arrowhead at the end so that it pointed toward the opposite side of the hourglass. "But if you give me enough time – and I happen to think there's something magic about seven years – I can begin to have complete certainty that I'll be doing what I want to do, where I want to do it, and with the kind of people I want to be doing it with."

Cheryl held up her empty glass to catch Sarah's attention, signaling that they needed refills on their Cokes. "That's the paradox of memories of the future, Charlie. You can be far more certain of your reality in the distant future than you can for the intervening five years or so, if you're willing to keep working, keep adjusting, and not quit," and with this she tapped Charlie's new eagle pin with her pen.

"Memories of the future?" Charlie asked with a quizzical smile.

"That's an FPN technique. We don't have time to go into the details right now, but basically it's a frequently replayed mental motion picture of your ideal future that is reinforced by continuous verbal affirmation and daily action."

"Wow!" Charlie drew out the word as if to emphasize how impressed he was. "You really are taking this business seriously, aren't you?"

"If I just blow it off, be satisfied to take whatever life tosses my way, and then one day wake up and decide I want more, will I be given the chance to do it over again?"

"No, of course not."

"Of course not, indeed! You're darned right I'm taking it seriously. I want magnificence, not mediocrity! There are just way too many things I want to do in this life. Which brings me to the next block of the Empowerment Pyramid," and she wrote into the next empty box in big block letters the word GOALS.

"Goals are the stepping stones that take you from where you are now to where you want to be in your perfect future. At FPN, we talk about the two possible impossibilities."

Charlie laughed incredulously. "First memories of the future and now possible impossibilities? I'm sorry, Cheryl, but FPN is beginning to sound more like a nuthouse than a business."

**The difference between courageous and crazy is often evident only in retrospect. It takes courage to commit yourself to the vision of a beautiful future, especially when everyone else thinks it's an impossible daydream.**

Cheryl smiled the smile of a mother trying to be tolerant when a child has asked "Why?" about ten times too many. "The difference between courageous and crazy is often evident only in retrospect, Charlie. It takes a lot of courage to commit yourself to a vision of a beautiful future, especially when everyone else thinks it's just an impossible daydream and that you're nuts for pursuing it."

"Yeah, I'm sorry," said Charlie, his contrition genuine. "My thinking's just been stuck in the corporate box for too long."

"You mean your dreams have been too small," Cheryl said as a statement rather than a question. "But at least I see the beginning of a crack at the top of that box. Maybe you're about to break out."

"Crazier things have happened."

"Let's hope so. The first possible impossibility is to have one magnificent dream, one goal that is so stupendous that other people think it's impossible."

"I remember reading once that lost causes are the only ones worth fighting for," Charlie said," and just then the picture of Mt.

Everest in Dick Dierdron's office popped into his head, with its inscription "Big Hills Are the Only Ones Worth Climbing."

"The second possible impossibility," Cheryl continued, "is to have an impossible number of possible goals. To write down everything you'd like to do, all the places you'd like to go, the people you'd like to meet. You'll find that when you start getting these goals organized, in your mind and on paper, the seemingly impossible becomes inevitable, and your goals start becoming fulfilled in big clusters. I know, because it's starting to happen to me right now, in my business and in my personal life. I'm achieving goals I never even would have thought to strive for if I hadn't written them down."

"One more thing about goals," Cheryl went on. "Whenever you begin an activity, have more than one goal in mind so that your likelihood of success is higher."

"I'm not sure I'm with you on that one," Charlie said. "Can you give me an example?"

"Sure," Cheryl replied. "Let's say you go somewhere for a job interview. What's your objective?"

"To get the job, of course. What else would it be?"

"If that's your only objective going in," Cheryl responded, "you're setting yourself up for a win or lose outcome. If you get the job you win – well, you win if it actually turns out to be what you're hoping it will be. But if you don't get the job, you feel like you've lost, because you didn't achieve your sole objective.

"If, on the other hand, getting the job is only one of several objectives, you set yourself up to win, no matter what the outcome is. You might not get the job, but you'll achieve your other objectives of learning more about the industry, getting names and telephone numbers for other people you can network with, and analyzing how your resume and your interview skills might have been more effective at helping you land the job. With all that to gain, you're a winner no matter what happens."

"Easy to say," Charlie replied, "but it's still hard to feel like a winner when you've been rejected."

"Look, I have a friend who's a writer. He told me he used to get really depressed whenever he went to a book signing. Because he's not – at least not yet, anyway – a household name, most people just walk by his table. He felt like he was being rejected by all of the people who didn't want his book. But now, he has multiple objectives at each signing. He asks the store manager for tips on how to market his books more effectively. He signs up new subscribers for his newsletter. And when people do stop, he engages them in conversations at a deeper level, asking about what they do and what their problems are. By doing that, he told me, he's always a winner. In fact, one of his most dismal outings, one where in an entire evening he signed only a few books, turned out to be one of his best because someone who did buy the book ended up hiring him several months later for a big consulting project. And as part of the deal, he bought more than a thousand books for employees of the company!

**Wishful thinking is hoping for something and waiting for it to happen. Positive thinking is *expecting* something and *working* to make it happen.**

"And that brings me to the apex of the pyramid," she said and blocked the word ACTION in the box at the top. "You can have all the beautiful dreams in the world, but they will only come true if you are willing to make the commitments and take the actions necessary to make them come true. The difference between wishful thinking and positive thinking is this: wishful thinking is hoping for something and waiting for it to happen. Positive thinking is *expecting* something and *working* for it to happen."

Charlie studied the Empowerment Pyramid. It really could, he realized, be a formula for finding out who you are, what you want, and how you're going to get it. "There's one more thing," said Cheryl, "and it's very important. Once you realize what your dreams and vision really are, you have to give yourself permission to follow those dreams, to become the person you were meant-to-be. You have to stop doing what you think the rest of the world expects you to do and trying to be the person everyone else expects you to be. The bigger your dream, and the more it requires you to change, the less likely that other people, including people who love and support you, are going to understand. Above all, you've got to believe in yourself and in your dreams before you can expect anyone else will."

Charlie contemplated what Cheryl had just said. To move from completing the Empowerment Pyramid on paper to making a real, here-and-now commitment, would require extraordinary courage and determination. The after-work crowd was starting to filter into The Patio when Cheryl excused herself for an early evening appointment. Charlie ordered another Coke and started making some notes for his own *Dreamcyclopedia*.

## CHAPTER THREE

# DREAM A BIG DREAM, MAKE IT A MEMORY OF THE FUTURE, AND EXPECT A MIRACLE

Charlie had never been this nervous before a meeting, not even one of the "paydirt presentations" at Logistics Precision, where his performance might be the difference between landing a big contract or landing in hot water. It was funny, he thought, because Alan Silvermane isn't even a "pay dust" meeting. No contract, no job offer would come from the meeting, since Silvermane was long-retired and no longer active with any of the businesses he'd help to build. He was meeting with Charlie as a favor to a friend.

"Most people don't want to be winners, because winning consistently would be inconsistent with their self-image of being survivors or victims." Charlie read that in an interview *Forbes* magazine had conducted several years earlier with Silvermane as part of their annual story on America's wealthiest people. Silvermane had ranked twenty-fifth that year. "Not bad for a kid who climbed down the steps of a boat from Europe in a rainstorm without even an umbrella," he had commented.

"In my experience," Charlie read Silvermane telling the reporter, "about 65 percent of the people in this country see themselves as survivors. They're tough and they'll make it through whatever the world throws at them, and if things get too bad, well, there's always the frontier, somewhere they can run away to and make a fresh new start." Charlie smiled – Silvermane had described his emotional reaction to losing the job with precision.

"Then there are the victims," Silvermane went on. "They constitute, oh, maybe 30 percent of the population. They can never seem to rise above their problems, but they always have someone to blame for those problems. Victims have no frontier to run away to, because they are stuck in the mud of their problems: boring jobs, toxic relationships, bankrupt finances." Charlie smiled, a bit more ruefully this time, at the uncomfortable recognition of himself in this description as well.

"That leaves something like 5-percent of the population – the winners who refuse to be made victims and who aspire to more than merely surviving – who aspire to carry the burden of creating wealth and progress."

That was the bad news, Silvermane concluded. The good news was that someone with a victim or survivor mindset could learn how to think and act like a winner. More important, he said, even a tiny increase in the proportion of Americans willing to take the risks and do the work required to be a winner could, in a short time, create millions of new jobs and add trillions of dollars to the nation's gross national product.

Charlie checked the clock. The cab would be here in an hour. He reviewed again the questions he wanted to ask Silvermane – mainly questions about dreaming big. "If my dreams are too small," he'd asked Cheryl, "then how do I learn to dream big? I don't even know where to start!" She thought for a moment then replied, "A friend of mine named Marv Johnston knows Alan Silvermane. You know, the guy who started the B-A-R Corporation when he was 24 and thirty years later sold it for more than 500 million dollars. Silvermane has been a mentor for some of the most successful entrepreneurs of our generation. When it comes to thinking big, he wrote the book. I'll see if I can make a connection for you."

The connection had been made, the cab ride completed, and now Charlie was sitting in Alan Silvermane's living room. It was nice, but nothing about it suggested it to be the home of one of America's most successful and wealthy businessmen. Silvermane had even answered his own door. Charlie had anticipated being greeted by a butler in white gloves who would escort him to a walnut paneled library.

They'd been speaking for almost an hour, and Charlie had yet to ask a question. The older man wanted to know everything about his guest. Charlie was having a hard time believing that the interest was real, that this billionaire who had been on the cover of every important business magazine would really care about the employment history, family, and the hobbies of a nobody like him (and then he immediately reminded himself to watch the negative self-talk). But Silvermane's attention never wavered; if anything, he seemed to be taking Charlie more seriously than Charlie took himself.

At length, Silvermane walked into the kitchen and returned with an elegant oriental tea pot and two cups and, after filling them both, gave one to Charlie. Then he leaned back into his chair and said, "Well, Marv said you had some questions for me, and so far I've done all the asking. Where do you want to start?"

Charlie sipped his tea. The eloquent opening lines he'd so carefully rehearsed had long since evaporated into the flow of conversation. "I'm not sure," he simply said. "Cheryl von Noyes – Marv's friend – tells me that my dreams are too small, that I've been cheating myself by pretending to be less that I really am, and by being satisfied with the accomplishment of pretty anemic goals. I suppose she's right. Right now, I'd fall somewhere between thinking of myself as a survivor and a victim on the scale you described in your Fortune interview."

Silvermane's reaction to the reference was barely noticeable, but he was obviously impressed that Charlie had done some homework. "Where do you want to fall on that scale, Charlie?" he asked, and without waiting for an answer continued: "It takes a lot of commitment, hard work, and sacrifice to move yourself up the food chain, but when you see the view from the top, you'll be thankful you made the climb, and you'll never want to go back down."

Charlie looked into his tea cup, saw a few shreds of tea leaf resting on the bottom, and suddenly became aware that his "little troublemaker" was creeping toward his mental swimming pool. "This guy thinks you're a loser," the troublemaker was saying. "Besides, if you try to climb that mountain, you'll probably fall and break your neck."

"You'll be surprised," Dr. Connors had told him, "how easy it is to chase the little troublemaker away, once you've recognized him."

"Beat it, punk!" Charlie could almost see the little brat up there with the startled expression of a kid who'd just been caught shoplifting, and then laughed at the imagined image of the little brat making a quick exit into the shadowed recesses of his mind.

"The first problem, Mr. Silvermane, is that I'm not really sure I want to climb a mountain at all. I guess I've gotten complacent hanging around down here in the valley and sort of look at myself as being too old to take up rock climbing. And even if I decided I wanted to climb a mountain, I don't have a clue which one I'd choose."

"Build your castles in the air, because that's where they belong. Then put foundations under them. Thoreau said that. I can't help you with the first question, Charlie. Whether or not you can generate the desire to achieve your dreams, once you know what they are, is between you and God. But maybe I can help you with the second one, because when it comes to deciding which mountain you wish to climb, or which castle to build, there are some general guiding principles."

Silvermane stood up again, and for a second Charlie thought he might push a button to unveil a blackboard hidden behind the paneling, so much like a teacher he sounded. Instead he walked over to a bookshelf and pulled down a fat notebook, which he opened to a page that was bookmarked with a protruding post-it note.

"My old friend John Marks Templeton was widely known, not only as a brilliant financial thinker, but also as a man whose unbridled optimism is fueled by a powerful faith in the hand of God working in this world. So when he predicted, back in 1992..." and here, Silvermane read from what appeared to be a newsletter stored in the binder, "that the Dow Jones Industrial Average may have reached six thousand, perhaps more, by the beginning of the 21st century, not very many people took him seriously. Most wrote it off as the wishful thinking of an incorrigible optimist."

Silvermane sat down with the notebook in his lap, and Charlie could see words and numbers scribbled all along the margins. "Do you follow the stock market, Charlie?"

"Not really," he replied, and felt a snicker from the little trouble-maker.

"Well, you should. Do you really think you can rely on those clowns in Washington to take care of your future?" He didn't wait for an answer, but continued, "Well, if you did follow the stock market you would know that the Dow surpassed the nine-thousand mark nearly two years before Sir John had predicted six-thousand. It reached fourteen-thousand several years ago. As you know, even if you don't follow the details, it has since taken some pretty steep dives and staged some pretty strong comebacks. The stock market will, as J.P. Morgan famously said, fluctuate and it takes courage to ride the rollercoaster. But if you can hang on, it's usually worth the ride. I'm telling you this, Charlie, because in many ways it's a metaphor for the decisions you face now. Over the long term, the upside potential is always much greater than the downside risk."

"That's the first of three paradoxes that occur when you set your sights on a big goal, one that ordinary people think of as impossible. What you stand to gain is so far out of proportion to what you might lose that even if you fail the first time, or the first ten times, if you keep at it the payback that always comes to those who don't quit will far more than make up for any losses you experience in getting there. And here's the kicker: the downside risk is usually the same no matter what the upside potential. You have to pledge your house to the bank to start a million dollar business or a hundred million dollar business, but you can only lose that house one time, can't you?"

Silvermane got up again and returned the notebook to the shelf. Charlie noticed a slight limp, and remembered having read that he chose to retire after having almost been killed in a skiing accident. "The second paradox is that audacious goals are more likely, not less likely, to be achieved than timid little ones. I'm a big supporter of Habitat for Humanity. Are you familiar with the organization?"

"More than I am with the stock market," Charlie replied with a smile.

"Well, then you know that Millard Fuller, the man who started it all, had this seemingly impossible goal of eradicating poverty housing everywhere in the world. That's quite a stretch, when you consider that there are over one billion people - four times the population of the United States - who are inadequately housed. But you know what? In its first twenty years, Habitat built more than 80,000 homes, and it only took another ten years for it to top a quarter-million." Silvermane stopped for a moment to let that thought sink in. "On that trajectory, you can actually see the day where the impossible dream of yesterday will be the reality of tomorrow."

Silverman crossed his arms and stretched his legs. "Now, if instead of targeting poverty housing around the world, Fuller had decided to start in his home state of Georgia, conquer the problem there, and then move on to South Carolina and so forth. Where would Habitat for Humanity be today?"

"Still in Georgia?"

"Precisely! It was the magnificence, the grandeur of the dream that propelled his efforts forward, that attracted the very resources necessary for the dream's fulfillment. If people only knew! Do you think that Millard Fuller worked 80,000 times harder than the well-intentioned social worker who spends a month trying to find decent housing for one family?"

"No, of course not."

"Of course not is right!" Silvermane nearly shouted the response in his excitement. Charlie was beginning to see why so many starting entrepreneurs came to him for guidance. "And though he himself has passed on to the next world, Habitat for Humanity is still a vibrant organization that is still changing the world. A great legacy is the ultimate payback of a big dream."

"Wanna know the third paradox?" Charlie nodded and Silvermane went on. "Audacious goals, castle in the sky dreams, are never just achieved. They are always transcended. They become the platform for bigger and better dreams, for the higher mountain in the distance that only becomes visible after you've peaked the ones in the foreground."

Silvermane was walking around again, as if his body didn't have the strength to hold down the irrepressible soul stored within.

"Back in the early '50s I was doing some work for Walt Disney. Talk about a big dreamer! Well, one day I was in his office and he was having a conversation with his brother Roy, who was sort of Walt's managerial counterweight. Walt was all excited about how wonderful this new theme park of his was going to be, but Roy looked like he'd just sat on a porcupine. Walt was seeing fairy castles in the air, and Roy was seeing a big hole in the ground into which he would have to pour their hard-earned money. At one point, he got real exasperated and just said, 'Walt, why can't you let go of this impossible dream for Disneyland and concentrate on making some money in the movie business?'"

Silvermane smiled, almost a surprised sort of smile, like he had just looked up and expected to see Walt and Roy instead of Charlie. "Well, of course we know what happened, don't we? Not only was Disneyland not an impossible dream, it wasn't even a particularly big dream, was it? Why, closing Disneyland tomorrow would hardly put a dent in balance sheet of the worldwide entertainment empire that started with the dreams of one man."

"Yeah, but big dreams cost a lot of money." The troublemaker, Charlie realized even as the words were coming out, had finally gotten to say something in this conversation.

"I'll tell you another paradox," Silvermane replied. "I've known some very big dreamers, very successful dreamers. Not one of them dreamed of money. Their dreams were always bigger than money. And not one of them *worried* about money. They had faith that as they progressed along the path toward their goals, the money they needed at each step would be there for them at the time they needed it. More than two thousand years ago the Taoist philosopher Chuang Tzu said that the only way to ever be truly happy is to not do anything that is calculated to make you happy. It's the same with money. If your only goal is having a lot of money, you probably never will. If your goal is something bigger, something you are fervently committed to, you'll find the money you need. And if you keep at it, someday you'll have more, maybe much more, than you need. But when you worry about where the money is coming from, you start to poison the dream."

Charlie nodded. "A friend of mine likes to say that worry is ingratitude to God – in advance."

"You have a very wise friend." Silvermane refilled the teacups. "You know what one of my big dreams is? To have a cup that keeps my tea at just the right temperature without having to wrap it in ugly plastic insulation or to cover it up with a lid with a tiny little sipping hole."

Charlie laughed. "Me too! Several years ago I took a ceramics class at the community college and made some cupholders that have a spot for a little tea candle underneath. They work great!"

Silvermane looked at the younger man, as if gauging the strength of a quality he had not yet detected. "Do you still have some of those cupholders?"

Charlie nodded. "They're not very attractive, but they serve the purpose."

"I wonder if you would send one my way. I'd love to keep my tea warm while I'm reading."

"Sure, no problem. In fact, I can drop one off tomorrow. With my current job, the hours are, you might say, flexible."

Silvermane laughed but his gaze never left Charlie. "Find a need and fill it. That's the best advice for people who have, uhm, flexible hours. And that's what you've just done, isn't it?"

"Well, I guess so, yeah."

"It wasn't that difficult, was it?"

Charlie smiled and shook his head. "It was also not a very big need."

"Neither is the chocolate chip cookie, but don't tell that to Mrs. Fields! "I'll tell you why big ambitious goals are more likely to succeed than timid little ones." Charlie pulled a pen and steno pad from his suit coat pocket, then looked to Silvermane as if for permission to make notes. "What I'm telling you is vitally important!" The older man exclaimed. "By all means, write it down!"

"A great big goal, a bet-the-company kind of goal, gives you four powerful tools that are not available with timid little goals. First, it's a magnet. When you're committed to a big goal – and I don't just mean it's something that you'd sort of like to do, but with an 'if it kills me' kind of commitment – it's a magnet that attracts the right people, the money, and everything else you need for its fulfillment."

"The second tool it gives you is a compass. When you've got your bearings fixed on a big mountain, you're much less likely to be drawn down all the little side paths of temptation. When you start to become massively successful," Silvermane looked at Charlie as if this were a given, "you'll have all sorts of opportunities to give speeches, sit on boards, and do a million other things that might stroke your ego but will pull you aside from the path toward the mountain. Your commitment to the goal will keep you on track."

"Third," he continued, "a big goal is a magnifying glass. We each have only so much time and energy, and when you have a huge goal you learn to focus it the way a magnifying glass pinpoints the sun's rays. You know, the average American spends twenty-five or thirty hours a week sitting in front of the boob tube; more than one third of their so-called free time is wasted on the trivial drivel that passes for entertainment. People with big dreams have more productive ways to engage their imaginations."

"Finally, a big dream is a flywheel. In your car's engine, the function of a flywheel is to maintain the crankshaft's momentum between each piston firing. That's what a big dream does. It keeps you going through the days when your pistons aren't firing, when you've been rejected one time too many, when one too many bill collector has threatened you with a collection agency, when but for your commitment to that dream, it would be so easy to quit." Silvermane chuckled. "To quit and get a job with more 'inflexible' hours."

**A big dream is a magnet, a compass, a magnifying glass, and a flywheel.**

Charlie smiled at the reference. He had a feeling that he would someday look back on this afternoon with Alan Silvermane as one of the most important in his life, yet if he'd still been working at LPI, he would never have allowed himself the time. He always had too much "work" to spare time for things that were important but not urgent, like learning from an old codger who would never be a customer.

As if in counterpoint to Charlie's thoughts, Silvermane said, "I hope I'm not boring you. Old fogies like me don't get much chance to share their wisdom. It seems like young people are always moving so fast these days."

"Not at all," Charlie responded as he finished writing something down in his steno pad. "I was actually trying to think of how I can use these tools in a practical way in my own situation."

"Well," Silvermane replied, "let me share one that's eminently practical but infinitely powerful. You've got to take your big dreams and transform them into memories of the future. Once you rely on that future memory the way you think you can rely on your past memories, your success becomes assured."

Charlie was surprised at the reference. "A friend of mine works for a group called Future Perfect Now, and memories of the future are one of the tools they use to motivate their people."

"Yes, I know. The founder of FPN has been, shall we say, a student of mine for a number of years. Memories of the future can be much more tangible and much more reliable than memories of the past. After all, for most of us our memory richly deserves the reputation it has earned for unreliability, doesn't it?"

"Well, yes."

"Well yes indeed! Let me illustrate. I would like for you to describe to me the events of your second birthday, in every detail. Tell me about the party, the gifts, the cake and the singing of the song, in every detail."

Charlie stared back blankly.

"What's the matter, Charlie, you did have a second birthday, didn't you?"

Charlie nodded.

"But you can't remember it! My point exactly. Now, tell me if you can close your eyes and picture where you're going to be in five minutes – who you'll be with, what you'll be wearing, even how tepid the tea you're drinking will be. Can you picture it?"

"Well of course," Charlie replied. "I'll be right here with you." With this teacup."

"Close your eyes and picture it," Silvermane commanded. "Can you see me and the room we're in clearly? Don't open your eyes yet, just concentrate on the picture. Can you see it?" Before he waited for Charlie to answer Silvermane said, "Now, can you hear in your mind what we're talking about, what my answers are to the questions you're about to ask? Can you hear me saying 'yes' to a request you've made for my help?"

"Sure. I can imagine that."

"You're doing more than imagining, Charlie. You're bringing it about. You have much more influence over the direction of the conversation than you imagine. Now, can you visualize a situation you will be in tomorrow?"

Charlie nodded in affirmation.

"Next week?"

Another nod.

"Next month? Next year? Five years from now? My experience with highly successful people is that they are very adept at 'remembering' something that will happen in the relatively distant future, and at being confident enough to rely on that memory. It gives them a greater store of faith to take necessary risks when they know how the story will turn out."

Silvermane set his teacup on the coffee table. "Most people think of time as a river flowing by, unstoppable and irreversible, a unidirectional current from future to past. I prefer to think of time as a lake, and my position on that lake as something over which I have a reasonable degree of control. Thus, if it helps me, I can paddle over to the end of the lake that other people think of as the future, build a dock to receive my boat when I return, and mark the path with buoys so that when I come back to the present, I will have a mental roadmap to guide me back to that dock, that memory of the future I've created in my mind."

The telephone on the desk by the window rang. Silvermane stared at it as though it were a telemarketer interrupting his dinner hour until it went silent, then returned his attention to Charlie. "All of the articles that have been written about me and my business success over the years missed the most important point. Not one of them said I was so successful simply because I knew where I was going, and I knew where I was going because I'd already been there. I guess their left-brained readers would have thought it was too weird, which is too bad, because it really works. Do you want to know how it works?"

"Yes, I do." Charlie answered, in truth anxious to learn how to use a technique that was beginning to make a lot of sense.

"An effective memory of the future has three components. First is a visual picture, and the more tangible and detailed, the better. Are you familiar with the notion of cognitive dissonance?"

Charlie nodded, saying, "It's when you try to hold two incompatible thoughts in your mind at the same time, like a cigarette company executive insisting that he's a good person who doesn't want kids to smoke, and at the same time knowing he has to use advertising to entice children to become replacement smokers for the older customers being killed off."

Silvermane nodded. "So what happens?"

"Something has to give. Either he blows the whistle or quits working for the tobacco company, or he deceives himself into believing that kids really don't pay attention to ads full of beautiful people pushing cigarettes, and that he's a good guy even though the product he's pushing kills lots of people."

"That's right," said Silvermane. "The same principle applies in creating memories of the future. If you have a vivid mental image of you as a successful entrepreneur living in a beautiful home, but the reality is that you're trapped in a job you hate, living in a crummy little apartment, something has to give. Either the picture decays into an idle daydream or vanishes altogether, or you figure out a way to start the business and move into the dream house."

Silvermane held one finger to each temple. "The neuro-psychologists at Stanford, where I went to business school, have shown that the subconscious mind is not able to distinguish between vivid imagination and reality. When you tenaciously hold a magnificent picture of a future reality in your mind, even when – *especially* when – it seems most unlikely to ever become real, your subconscious mind starts to work round-the-clock to create what it believes *should* be your reality. I'll tell you, some of my best ideas for achieving my own dreams have come to me through my dreams at night, or those sudden 'A-Ha!' epiphanies you get walking out in the country, when the subconscious mind is liberated and can guide you toward the creation of what you have caused it to believe should be your reality!

"So the first element of a memory of the future is a mental picture. The second is verbal affirmation, because while we dream in pictures, we tend to worry in words. You'll have a mental picture of this beautiful new house in your mind, and that nagging little voice of doubt will say, 'You can't afford the mortgage you have now! How are you gonna pay for that monstrosity?' That's when you need to remind yourself with affirmations that you are capable of achieving your goals and that you deserve to enjoy the fruits of your success. Shakespeare said that your doubts can be traitors by keeping you from taking the actions that could bring you victory. That's why you have to make your doubt work for you, not against you. When it says 'You can't do that,' you need to ask, 'Why not?' and 'What do I have to do to make it possible. That way you make your doubt start knocking down the excuses, one-by-one."

Silvermane laughed as if some ancient memory had reached out from the past and tickled his funny bone. "Remember the guy who made millions selling those office volcanoes?"

Charlie wasn't sure whether or not to admit to having bought one. "You mean the little clay mountain with an indentation on top for lighting one of those charcoal snakes the kids always get on the Fourth of July?"

"That's the one." Silvermane was still laughing. "Hank Patton – he's the guy who thought up the idea – why, at first he could hardly give the things away. Then he came up with that magnificent advertising slogan – *Fire Up Your Office* – and the things started to fly off the shelves. It almost didn't happen, though. You see, Hank had a serious self-esteem problem. Every time he started making progress, he would do some foolish thing that would set him back financially, antagonize a key customer, one thing after another. He had a real fear of success, if you want to know the truth of it."

Silvermane smiled and shook his head. "I was on his board back then and tried to convince him to get some counseling, but he wouldn't hear of it. It was a macho thing, you know. But one thing I did get him to do was change the way he talked to himself. He'd always been such a pessimist, expecting that the bank would call his loan, or that a big customer would back out of a deal, and so on. And of course, he seemed to have more than his share of that kind of problem."

"Well, one day after a board meeting where he'd been particularly pessimistic, I asked him if he talked to himself the same way he talked to us. 'What do you mean?' he asked, like I was, you know, implying he was crazy or something. But when I explained what

I was talking about, he said 'Heck NO! I give you guys the sugar-coated version. In my own mind I assume that everything will turn out worse than you could ever imagine. That way I can be ready for every possible disaster.'

"Well, Charlie, I don't need to tell you I was horrified by his response. No wonder we were having so many disasters! Old Hank was conjuring them up in this mind, and once something becomes clear enough in your mind, you can be sure you'll see it with your eyes before very long."

"What did you do?" Just that morning, Charlie had been imagining a fight with LPI over his severance agreement, getting rejected by every company where he'd applied for a job, and having the bank cancel his personal line of credit now that he was starting to use it.

"It took some convincing, but over the next couple of months, I got Hank to change his inner scripts. Guess what? Within about three months, we stopped having a disaster every other week, and the company's sales started to take off. We really didn't do a whole lot different, other than change the way Hank talked to himself. Now he's become such a big believer that he puts everyone who comes into the company – *everyone*, from janitors to vice-presidents – through a course on visualization and self-talk. As a result, his company has been on the *Inc.* magazine list of the fastest growing companies for the past several years."

Charlie was silent so Silvermane went on. "Did you know it's a documented fact that the human mind, left to its own devices, will automatically gravitate toward negative, frightening and depressing thoughts? That's why it's so important for you to pay attention to your self talk. You have to override a lot of obsolete mental programming – the fight or flight reflex and so on – with positive expectations. And the way you do that is by talking to yourself."

**You have to override obsolete mental programming with positive expectations. And the way you do that is by talking to yourself.**

Charlie thought for a moment then said, "I imagine it's most important to talk to yourself in a positive way at those times when it seems hardest to do – when you've been rejected at every turn and you're running out of money and feel like a failure." As he waited for Silvermane's response he silently repeated one of the affirmations he'd written for himself after his last meeting with Cheryl: "I am a winner, and I will turn every rejection into a future success. I will have the money I need at the time I need it, and when I am focused on my true mission, I will not be allowed to fail." It felt good to hear it inside his head, and he sat up a little straighter in his chair. "You said there were three components to a memory of the future. Mental visualization and verbal affirmations are the first two. What's the third?"

"Action!" Silvermane slapped the palm of his hand down on the coffee table, rattling the tea cups in their saucers. "Action. Without consistent, daily action that moves you in the direction of your goals, it's not a dream, it's just a daydream." Silvermane let that sink in for a moment. "I've already talked about some of the tools that big ambitious goals give you. I should also mention three incredible mental resources you have at your disposal, ready to be fired up as soon as you commit to your dream. These resources," he said, pointing to Charlie's steno pad as if to tell him that he should be writing this down, "are all-powerful. I once had the privilege of meeting the late Napoleon Hill. He wrote one of the all-time classic self-help books, *Think and Grow Rich*. Have you read it?"

"A long time ago," Charlie muttered, not looking up from his steno pad.

"Well read it again, and do it soon. You're at a critical juncture where a little bit of thinking could redirect you in some very productive ways. Anyway, Mr. Hill told me that most people had it backwards. The average person believes he doesn't have time to think because he's too busy trying to make a living. Why, he was just downright indignant about it. 'I didn't write a book called *Grow Rich and Think* for a reason,' he told me. 'If only people would use their minds.' We have this incredible mental resource, but most people turn it off the minute they turn their television sets on."

Silvermane pointed to his head again. "That's where the buried treasure is, Charlie. Right up here. You've got three precious resources that can help you attain any goal. The first is your attention. You know, people have no idea what a precious gift they are requesting when they ask someone for their attention. In many respects, it's all you have. It's a much more limited and valuable commodity even than time. The most important decisions you make have to do with what you pay attention to. Do you pay attention to bad news or good news? Do you pay attention to TV or great books? Do you pay attention to problems and scarcity or opportunities and abundance?"

"I'd never really thought of attention that way," Charlie said, underlining something in his pad, "as your most precious resource. Maybe that's why people say *pay* attention."

"I'm sure you're right. Your attention account cannot be overdrawn, ever. The second mental resource you have," Silvermane went on, once again pointing to Charlie's pad to indicate that he should be writing this down, "is your imagination. It's such a precious gift, imagination, but most people abuse theirs. They either squander it away conjuring up lurid images of a horrible future they would never want to see – in other words, worry – or dreaming up beautiful pictures of an ideal existence that they have no intention whatsoever of trying to bring about – daydreaming."

Silvermane paused as Charlie caught up on his note-taking. "Now, a little bit of worry and a little bit of daydreaming can be good things, but the most productive use of your imagination is creating memories of the future. It's the difference between Walt Disney building Cinderella's castle in the air and then laying a foundation under it, and the average Joe coming home at night, plopping down in front of the tube with a beer, and dreaming about winning the lottery so he'll never have to work again. Of course, when he's done fantasizing, he starts to worry again, because his problems are still there biting him on the ankles since he hasn't been thinking about how to solve them."

They had been speaking for over three hours now, and Silvermane showed no signs of fatigue. If anything, his energy and enthusiasm were growing as he went on. "The other thing about imagination is that the more you use it, the more you feed it information from many different areas, the more you stretch it and work it by transforming ideas into real things, the more it will mature into intuition. You have this imaginary dream in your head, and your intuition will start to lead you toward the people you need to see and the actions you need to take in order to make that dream become real."

"Your third mental resource," he continued, "is belief. Belief is the essential catalyst that transforms a dream into a memory of the future. I called the first company I ever started the B-A-R Corporation. Not very many people have asked me what the letters stood for, but they were an ongoing reminder to me – Believe, Achieve, Receive. That's something else most people have backwards. They want someone else to give them something – money, recognition, whatever – before they've earned it. Then they figure they'll go out and achieve something, because now they have the resources and the confidence to do it without taking too many uncomfortable risks. Then, only after they see everything starting to fall in place, will they really believe that this good thing is happening."

Charlie finished writing, and when it was evident Silvermane had concluded, asked a question: "You used the term 'fear of success' a while ago. I'd never really thought about it. I mean, why would anyone be afraid of something we all say we want more of? But several people have used that term lately. What's your take on it?"

"Good question. In my opinion, it's the biggest single obstacle facing anyone who sets their sites on building a business. There are two parts to it. First, most of us have a sneaking suspicion that we don't deserve success. It's a combination of low self esteem and ambivalence about money. We're taught from a very early age to not stand out – to not be a teacher's pet or an apple-polisher – and that there's something vaguely wrong with having more than enough for yourself when there are people starving in India. You have to really believe that God wants you to be a rip-roaring success, and then be committed to sharing your success with other people.

"Second, people fear the consequences of success. They're more worried about what they might lose than what they could gain.

They suspect, quite correctly, that success brings in its train a whole new set of obligations, that instead of being able to coast and spend their days smelling the roses, they're going to become indentured to all the people who helped them climb the ladder to success."

"So how do you overcome the fear of success?" Charlie asked.

"You have to dream beyond the dream," Silvermane replied.

"Pardon me?"

"People today are too short-term in their orientation. They aren't willing to concentrate on one thing for an extended period of time, to the exclusion of everything else. They want instant gratification."

Charlie laughed, and when the older man paused, not thinking he'd said something funny, Charlie said, "I'm sorry, but your comment just reminded me of a recent conversation I had with my 14-year-old daughter. I asked her if she understood the concept of delayed gratification. 'Well,' she replied, 'I think I know what delay means, and I certainly understand the concept of gratification, but when you bring them together it's a…' Then she stopped and asked, 'Dad, what's that word you like to use when two concepts don't go together? It sounds like a stupid cow?"

"Oxymoron," Silvermane interjected, and both men laughed at the little girl's imagination. "Yes, but it's not just your daughter's generation, it's also her parents' generation that thinks there's something slightly moronic about putting off the many little instant gratifications so they can someday have the one big one. The paradox – there's another great word for your daughter; tell her it's a pediatrician and a cardiologist having lunch together. There paradox is that once they achieve that one big gratification that they've worked so hard and waited so long for – all manner of other opportunities to do exciting and wonderful things that never before would have been possible come in its wake. If you want to be happy in the long run, it usually means denying yourself all sorts of opportunities to have fun in the short run."

Silvermane stood up and walked over to the mantle above his fireplace. "I've won many awards and been given many honors in my day. Most of them are packed away in boxes somewhere, but

I keep an important reminder up here." He picked up a picture frame, one of those triptych frames holding three leaves together so it could be folded up like a book, and held it open in front of him, looking from one page to another.

"There are three documents in this frame, Charlie. One is the incorporation certificate for my first company, dated from 1949. I had just finished college, and had set my mind on becoming a millionaire within two years. Pretty ambitious, no? The second is a 1954 letter from a creditor threatening me with a lawsuit if I didn't pay an overdue bill that I had no way of paying at that time. So much for being a millionaire in two years! The third is a little handwritten note from my accountant, dated 1962. It's short, so I'll read it to you. It says, 'Congratulations, Al! I've just completed your tax returns for the year and you are now officially a millionaire.' That's all. Want to know what I did when I got that note?"

"Celebrated?"

"Nope. I stuck it in my drawer and got back to work. I'd long since outgrown that goal. When it finally happened, it was no longer a goal, just a necessary waystation along the path to something bigger. Here's another paradox. Had I not outgrown that goal, I never would have achieved it. That's why you have to dream beyond the dream. As you grow, your old dreams get proportionately smaller. They stop inspiring you."

Silvermane replaced the picture frame. "I'll tell you why I didn't achieve that first goal of becoming a millionaire in record time. It was a false goal. Never frame your dreams, the ones that really count, in terms of money. Have a bigger dream than a pile of money and the money will be there as you need it. If all you dream of is having a pile of money, you never will, but you will have a heart full of worry. People think all their problems would go away if a dumptruck would just come up and unload a small mountain of money in their front yard. Actually, the only thing money does is give you the right to graduate to bigger and more interesting challenges than the problems you're facing right now."

"That's why you have to dream beyond the dream," Silvermane repeated. As he said that, he stood up in a clear indication that the interview was coming to a close. "If there's an endpoint to your dream, like having a million dollars in the bank, even if it does happen, which is unlikely, you won't keep it for very long. As soon as you stop striving toward the big goal far in front of you, you start slipping backwards."

As the two men shook hands Charlie said, "Thanks, Mr. Silvermane, you've given me a lot to think about."

**You have to dream beyond the dream. As soon as you stop striving toward the big goal far in front of you, you start slipping backwards.**

Silvermane smiled. "Charlie, it's too early for you to start thinking. You'll just think your way back into the same old box. Now is the time for you to be *dreaming*! Big, heroic dreams. Mountain-sized dreams! Thinking is the tool by which you chisel those mountains down into magnificent works of art. But first, you must choose the right mountain."

CHAPTER FOUR

# Stop Worrying So You Can Start Winning

"You look worried again, Charlie. What is it this time?"

It took Charlie a moment to reorient himself from the inner world in which he'd been mentally wandering back to the outer world through which he was now walking. Emerging from the deep pit of his anxieties into the magnificent cathedral of the Grand Canyon took his breath away. The desert breeze played softly through his hair as the sun warmed his face, sending a tingle down his spine. Even after four days of hiking, Charlie was still overwhelmed by the vast splendor of this greatest of all places for spiritual awakening.

"Did you see the bighorn sheep looking down at us from the butte back half a mile or so? Or that pair of hawks circling the pinnacle across the river?"

Mitch Matsui had been one of Charlie's best friends since their days at St. Johns. He was the class philosopher, and over the years Charlie had always consulted with him on important decisions. After school, Mitch had passed up many lucrative opportunities in the business world to stay on and teach at the college.

If his classmates had ever felt sorry for Mitch struggling to get by on a teacher's salary, they didn't anymore. His first book of poetry, *Live Your Dreams Before They Come True,* was an international bestseller, as were the sequels, and he now had more invitations for speaking engagements than he could possibly accept. Through all his success, Mitch remained the humble philosopher he'd always been. He didn't even take credit for the book. "I was just lucky enough to be the official translator for the poetry of McZen," he'd say, though no one really believed that McZen was anything other than a figment of Mitch's imagination.

It had been Mitch's idea to go hiking in the Grand Canyon. Charlie was struggling with whether to follow his dreams and go into business for himself or to give in to his fears and doubts and get a "real job." Mitch suggested that a week in the desert would help him focus on his priorities.

"Well?" Like an alarm clock coming back to life after the snooze button had timed out, Mitch again dragged Charlie away from his inner thoughts. "What are you worrying about this time? What mental weight is so heavy that it's keeping you from appreciating..." and here Mitch simply spread his arms as if to symbolically capture the grandeur that stretched out in every direction.

"Oh, nothing," Charlie replied. "I was just thinking about how my being unemployed has affected my family."

Mitch took several steps off the trail and picked up a chunk of granite that Charlie guessed weighed nearly a pound. He tossed it up and down a few times, as though weighing it, then said, "This seems to be about the right size for that worry."

Mitch walked over to Charlie and unzipped the lower compartment of his backpack. "Oh man," Charlie groaned, "I don't need to carry another rock!"

"You certainly don't," Mitch agreed, "which makes me wonder why you go out of your way to pick them up." Mitch put the rock in Charlie's backpack, jamming it sideways into the small quarry that had been gradually accumulating over the past several days.

At the start of their trek, Charlie had agreed to go along with one of Mitch's wild ideas. Every time he caught Charlie worrying, Mitch would pick up a stone and put it into his friend's backpack. Carrying those rocks around would be a metaphor for the emotional weight of all of the worries with which Charlie had burdened himself. Now, Charlie regretted the decision. His shoulders ached under the burden of more than 20 rocks of various sizes, and each new stone seemed disproportionately heavier than previous rocks of the same size. While Mitch bounded across the trail as though his backpack was filled with helium balloons, Charlie felt like one of the pack mules they'd seen laboring down the trail on the first day.

Mitch zipped Charlie's backpack shut and gave it a whack. "Let's go, my friend," he said. "A few more hours and we'll stop for lunch. Then we'll have a cairn ceremony."

"A what?"

"It's time to take some of the weight off your shoulders," Mitch replied, "both physically and metaphorically. I'll explain how it works at lunch."

Mitch speeded on ahead, telling Charlie he had to make preparations for the ceremony. Before they parted, he extracted from Charlie a promise that any time he caught himself worrying, he himself would pick up another rock and add it to the collection in his pack. Motivated by this promise, for the next three hours Charlie kept his eyes on the scenery about him and his mind on each step in front of him. Paying attention to every step, he felt more light-footed; even his pack seemed to lose a little weight.

At last, Charlie saw Mitch sitting by the side of a small stream. He could see that lunch was already prepared, and also that Mitch had cleared a small area on the ground. With a surge of gratitude, he dropped his heavy pack, retrieved his water bottle, doused his face and then his thirst. During lunch, neither man said much. Afterward, Mitch asked Charlie to bring all of the rocks out of his backpack and lay them out on the ground. "Look at all these worries," Mitch exclaimed. "No wonder you always feel so weighed down!"

"It's a lot easier to carry around the ones you can't see," Charlie replied.

"Is it really?" Mitch pushed one of Charlie's rocks with his walking stick. "It seems to me that the mental rocks can be a lot heavier than the physical ones. They certainly take a greater toll, and can be a lot harder to leave behind."

"I guess I'd have to agree with that," Charlie responded. As he looked at the pile of rocks, he wished that it was as easy to empty his mind of worries as it had been to empty his backpack of rocks.

"How do you define worry?" Mitch asked.

"I really hadn't thought about it," Charlie replied. "I guess it's thinking about bad things that might happen in the future."

Mitch smiled and shook his head. "That's probably what 99 out of 100 people would say, and it's OK as far as it goes, but not nearly enough. If you want to beat the worry habit – and it is a habit, a really bad habit – the first step is to understand what worry really is, and what it does to you. Until you stop worrying, you can't start winning."

Mitch picked up one of Charlie's rocks and gazed into it as though it were a crystal ball. "The more you dissipate your mental and emotional energy on worry, the less likely you are to see the opportunities you have for achieving your goals, and to find the courage and perseverance it takes to live your dreams. Actually, I have many definitions for worry. Some of them may surprise you. Like this one: Worry is a money repellent."

**The more you dissipate your mental and emotional energy on worry, the less likely you are to see the opportunities you have for achieving your goals, and to find the courage and perseverance it takes to live your dreams.**

"What do you mean, it's a money repellent?" Charlie asked as he watched Mitch pick up one of the rocks he'd dumped out of his backpack and put it in the center of the small space he had cleared out.

"Just that," replied Mitch. "If there's something you really want to get done – more than that, it's something you feel you *must* get done, you'll find the money. Somehow, money arrives in just the right increments at just the right time." Mitch picked up another of Charlie's rocks and set it down next to the first one. "As soon as you start *worrying* about how you're going to pay for the project, you've taken the first step to killing it."

"That's ridiculous," retorted Charlie. "How can worrying about money drive money away?"

"I'll tell you how. When you worry about money, you're seeing the world as a place of scarcity. On the other hand, when you trust that the money you need will come when you need it, you're seeing the world as a place of abundance. Money flows to people with an abundance mentality, and it flees from people with a scarcity mentality. In our entrepreneur's club, we read the book *Think and Grow Rich* by Napoleon Hill. Well, he didn't call it *Worry and Grow Rich* for the good reason that you're more likely to worry yourself into the poor house than you are to worry yourself into a mansion."

Charlie shook his head in disagreement. "Then how come so many wealthy people still worry so much about money?"

Mitch picked up another rock and laid it in the clearing. "To have a great deal of money does not make one wealthy; to be wealthy is to not worry about money. McZen said that broke is a state of wallet; poverty is a state of mind."

Mitch held an open hand out toward the rocks that had been dumped from Charlie's backpack. "Many of these rocks, these worries, that you've been carrying around for the past four days are about money. Has all that worrying made you any wealthier?"

Charlie looked sheepishly at the rocks, then replied, "No, of course not. But every time I think about starting my own business, it worries me that I don't have enough of a safety net."

Mitch smiled and laid a rock on top of those that were already stacked in his little clearing. "You'd worry a lot less about having a safety net if you would appreciate how close to the ground your tightrope really is. What's the worst thing that can happen if you fall off, if you start a business and it fails? Will they put you in debtors' prison, or make you work as a galley slave to pay your debts off?"

"Of course not," Charlie snorted. "They haven't done those things for centuries."

"So what is the absolute worst thing that can happen?" Mitch persisted.

"Well," Charlie replied, "I'm sure declaring bankruptcy is no walk in the park!" Now Charlie picked up one of his rocks and added it to the pile Mitch had started.

"Certainly not," said Mitch, "but it's not the end of the world either. Pick up any issue of *Success* or *Entrepreneur* magazine, and you'll read about somebody who has overcome bankruptcy and gone on to great success and wealth."

"I know, Mitch, but after so many years of having a real job with a regular paycheck, the insecurity of entrepreneurship is disconcerting."

Mitch laughed softly. "Here's something else McZen said: Someone with a job is never secure; someone with a calling is never unemployed." Charlie remembered Cheryl having quoted that line, and her comment that it had forever changed her perspective on work.

Mitch picked up the granite one-pounder, which was the last rock he'd stuffed into Charlie's backpack and again tossed it up and down in his hand, taking it's measure. "In today's world, no job will give you security; and no paycheck is big enough to relieve you of money worries. Try to think of a job that would give anyone permanent security," Mitch challenged.

"Neurosurgeon," Charlie replied with defiance.

"Yeah? You know what they call a neurosurgeon in Philadelphia today?" Charlie shrugged. "Hey, waiter!" Mitch yelled, pantomiming the act of summoning a waiter in a crowded restaurant. They both laughed, and Mitch continued, "I know a lot of doctors who are living from paycheck to paycheck. They make a lot, but they also spend a lot. They worry about managed care and medicare, about how they're viewed and about being sued." When Charlie rolled his eyes at the awkward rhyme, Mitch laughed and said, "What do you expect? I translate poetry for a living."

Now Mitch became serious. "The only employment security in the world today is loving your work, and doing it with confidence and enthusiasm. If your work is a calling and not just a job, you'll be as busy as you want to be."

Mitch dropped the granite rock onto the growing pile. "Many people are trapped in what I call the Wu Ch'i paradox. Wu Ch'i lived during the Warring States period of Chinese history, nearly 2,500 years ago. He wrote that on the battlefield, those who are determined to die with glory will live, while those who merely hope to escape with their lives will die. It's the same in the world of business. If your only goal is to retire with a big nest egg, you'll never make it. On the other hand, if you have a passion for changing the world and you attack your cause like a true crusader, the nest egg will take care of itself."

Mitch placed another stone on the pile. "A cairn is a pile of rocks that a traveler builds to show the way for those who come behind. If you keep your eyes open, Charlie, you'll find that the world is full of cairns – guideposts that will assuage your anxiety and direct you down the path towards success. That's what we're doing on this trip. We're building a set of guideposts that can help you avoid being paralyzed by your worries. For example, here's a guidepost to help you stop worrying about money problems: Commit yourself to making the personal changes that are needed to help you increase your earning capacity, and to reduce your material desires until after those changes have been made. The essence of entrepreneurship is creating lasting economic value for yourself and others. No matter how much you get paid, as long as you're working on a per hour basis you've only got a job or – how does Cheryl put it? You've got a J-O-B and might end up jilted, obsolete, and broke."

Charlie propped his elbows up against his backpack and leaned back, savoring the warmth of the midday sun. "You know what would be the worst thing about bankruptcy? Even worst than losing your possessions?" Mitch cocked his head expectantly, so Charlie continued. "It would be the humiliation of it all. The way old friends would avoid you on the street, and the way all those people who told you to forget the entrepreneur thing and just get a real job would be gloating how they told you so. I could just imagine people telling their children to work harder in school so they don't end up like poor old bankrupt Charlie McKeever!"

Mitch added another rock to the cairn. "You know, Charlie, you'd worry a lot less about what other people think of you if you'd appreciate how infrequently they think of you." Charlie laughed, but didn't seem very convinced. "Think about it," Mitch continued, "of all the people you know, how many have crossed your mind in the past hour? In the past day or week?" Charlie laughed and shook his head. "And all those people that you haven't been thinking of? They haven't been thinking of you either. So why waste your time worrying about what you think they think of you when they're not thinking of you at all."

They sat in silence for several minutes before Mitch spoke again. "You have to manage your thinking, you can't just let it flow spontaneously. Your conscious mind is like water. Left unattended, it naturally flows downhill, into the ruts and potholes of worry, fear, and depression, where it will stay until you do something to pump it back out. That is the natural tendency of ego. Only by your deliberate effort can you pipe your thinking out of the ruts and up to the mountaintops of equanimity, daring, and joy."

Mitch was sitting cross-legged, using his packed-up sleeping bag as a cushion. "You're in real danger when you let your ego start making decisions for you, Charlie. Your ego wants you to believe that you are the center of the universe, which is a pretty laughable concept when you look around at the magnificent sculptures in this canyon, which God has been working on for millions of years. How many people do you know who every day get up before they want to, rev themselves up with a pot of coffee, and then head off to a job they don't like, but keep doing that job because they need the money and the status to please or impress other people?"

Charlie squeezed his eyes shut, and focused on the psychedelic images that were swirling, red and orange, behind his eyelids as the sun refused to be shut out. Mitch had just described his own life for at least the past five years at LPI. "It's funny, Mitch, but just about everyone I've talked to in the past month has come back to ego as if it were a big wall standing between you and your dreams."

Mitch leaned forward and rummaged through the remaining rocks, finally picking up an ugly brown one, the biggest of the lot, and placed it atop the cairn. "Worry is the natural state of ego. When you worry about something, it makes you feel important – like if something bad happens to you the universe will somehow be a diminished place. Furthermore, ego is basically lazy; it's a lot easier to worry about a problem than it is to do the work required to fix the problem, and ego would rather worry than work. Have you ever noticed how, no matter what it is you're doing, it always seems like there's something more urgent you should be doing?"

Charlie opened his eyes and smiled. "With the exception of this very moment, that's been pretty much a chronic situation for my whole life."

"Put another rock on the cairn, Charlie. That's just another form of ego-based worry. Ego gains a sense of importance by having so many seemingly urgent things to do. By worrying about your problems all at once, it never has to get around to actually doing anything about them. Ego loves to be in that situation – all worry and no work."

Charlie shook his head. "You talk about ego as if it's some sort of alien body. But it's an essential part of who I am, isn't it? And isn't it good to have a strong ego?"

"Of course," replied Mitch. "Ego is just a word, a construct, to describe a deeper underlying reality. And that reality is often one of inner conflict – as when you try to decide between doing what you think you want to do and what you think other people expect you to do. Boiled down to its essence, it's the age-old conflict between ego and soul."

After skipping a rock across the little stream, Mitch screwed the top off his nalgene bottle and took a drink, then laid another of Charlie's rocks on top of the cairn. "They are always in conflict, ego and soul. When you're worried and agitated, ego is in control. When you're at peace and feeling a sense of faith, you know soul is at the wheel." Mitch had picked up another rock and was tossing it back and forth between his two hands as he spoke. "Ego seeks security; soul seeks adventure. Ego wants things; soul wants experiences. Ego wants friends; soul wants to be a friend. Ego is a hanging on; soul is a letting go. Ego is anxiety; soul is faith."

Mitch scooped up the remaining rocks from Charlie's backpack, and laid them at his feet. "Here's another definition: Worry is an abuse of your imagination. Instead of using your imagination to dream up a beautiful future, you use it to manufacture nightmares – imaging awful things that you don't want to have happen. Worry is also a wet blanket that suffocates intuition. When you worry, you lose access to your natural-born intuitive intelligence. And worry is the stepchild of anxiety."

Clenching both hands into fists, Mitch placed one against each temple and made a grinding motion. "Anxiety is an emotional vice. It is the mortal foe of creative thought and decisive action. When you're full of anxiety, two bad things happen to shut down imagination and intuitive intelligence. First, your perceptions of reality are distorted, as if you are looking at the world, and yourself, through a funhouse mirror. When you're full of anxiety, problems always seem bigger and more intractable than they really are, and your own resources and strengths seem a lot smaller and more insignificant than they really are.

"The second bad thing that happens is that you simply do not see options that would be available to you if, rather than being filled with worry and anxiety, you were full of faith and confidence. There is always something to worry about, and worry is a natural human condition. The challenge is to replace *worrying* about problems with *thinking* about solutions; to replace *worrying* about future dangers with *thinking* about how to prevent them. The challenge is to change the subject; to stop worrying about how hard life is, and instead to focus on what you must do to effectively meet the challenges."

**The challenge is to replace *worrying* about problems with *thinking* about solutions; to replace *worrying* about future dangers with *thinking* about how to prevent them.**

Mitch put the last rock on top of the cairn and brushed the dust from his hands. "That's quite a respectable little pile we've built here, isn't it? When we start walking again, we'll leave all of these rocks behind. Maybe they'll help someone else find the path to equanimity. And maybe, as we walk off, you can leave behind the worries that each one of those rocks represents. You move a lot faster when you travel light!"

"I wish it was that simple," Charlie replied, staring at the pile of rocks.

"It is that simple," Mitch said. "Simple, but not easy." Mitch leaned forward and uncurled his legs, propping his forearms on his knees to lean in Charlie's direction. "How long have you been down here in the Grand Canyon?"

Charlie shrugged his shoulders. "Same as you, Mitch. About four days."

"No, Charlie, up until now most of the time we've been walking, your mind has been somewhere else." Mitch laughed and pointed at Charlie. "You've been having an extended out-of-body experience! Your body is down here in the Grand Canyon. But your mind is who-knows-where doing who-knows-what. I've been down here for four days, but I doubt that you've really been here more than about four hours. Am I right?"

Charlie smiled and shook his head. "Guilty as charged."

"That's the secret to overcoming worry, Charlie. Keep your mind and your body in the same time zone. Almost all emotional pain is caused by time travel—either guilt, regret and anger from the past or fear and anxiety about the future. When you keep your attention anchored in the present, you can start to break the worry habit. That's why McZen said to live your dreams before they come true—just in case you never wake up. The images you run through your mind today will profoundly influence the outcomes you get in the future. If you spend a lot of time worrying that your kid will turn into a juvenile delinquent, the worry itself can cause you to act in ways that actually bring it about. On the other hand, if you have faith that your children will turn out fine, even as they go through adolescent rough spots, chances are that's what will end up happening."

The two men packed their gear and resumed their trek, leaving behind the cairn piled with Charlie's worry stones. For several hours, the silence was interrupted only by the crunching of their boots on the rock path and the occasional squawk of a raven. At length Mitch said, "I said that breaking the worry habit was simple but not easy. We've covered the simple part – to keep your attention in the present and stop being so concerned about pleasing and impressing other people. If you'd like, I can share with you some of the practical action steps that have helped me break out of the worry habit."

"I'd like that a lot," Charlie replied.

"As I said, it's simple but not easy. You have to discipline yourself. And the first step is to take care of your physical body. Descartes was wrong when he said that mind and body are totally separate; what happens in one profoundly influences the performance of the other. Besides being tired and sore, how have you felt the past few days – I mean emotionally?"

Charlie took a breath and stretched his shoulders back. "Remarkably great!"

"Part of the reason," said Mitch, "is that you're taking care of your body's four essential needs. First is simply to get enough sleep. When you cheat yourself on sleep, your mind is much more prone to worry and anxiety attacks. Out here on the trail, there's nothing to do after the sun goes down – no TV, no refrigerator, no evening newspaper. So we talk for a while, then go to sleep, at an hour probably much earlier than you're used to. Am I right?"

"Yep, and you know what? I really haven't missed those late night TV shows – not even the news. Especially not the news."

"The second thing you've been doing," Mitch went on, "is getting proper nutrition. You scowled at me when I gave you a baggie full of pills for each day of the trip, but taking that daily dosage of vitamins and minerals has given you greater physical energy, which in turn builds your emotional fortitude."

"And you know what?" Charlie asked. "Taking those pills really isn't so bad, once you get used to it."

"Especially if you take them with water," Mitch laughed, "and that's something else that's very important. Ironically, I'll bet that out here in the desert environment of the Grand Canyon you're better hydrated than you are back at home. That's because we're paying attention to our water needs, and not filling up on all those caffeinated drinks that get you dehydrated even as they seem to quench your thirst. So the third thing to keep doing when you get back is drinking plenty of water during the day. The fourth thing you're doing, quite obviously, is getting exercise – probably a lot more than you're used to getting."

"Now there's the understatement of the trip," laughed Charlie, "although it feels a lot better now that I'm not carrying half the rocks in this canyon in my pack!"

"If you read all the books on how to overcome depression and anxiety," Mitch continued, "one of the common themes will be to get physical exercise. This is important for two reasons. First, the exercise itself is a safe release for the stress that can create physical and emotional problems. Second, when your body is strong, you're better able to cope with the daily demands that can seem so stressful."

They walked on in silence for a while longer, when Mitch stopped and pulled the topographical map out of his pack. "I'm about to demonstrate something else that's important to controlling your worry, and that is to train your doubt. It's advice from the great German poet Rilke: doubt can be paralyzing, but you can train it by forcing it to ask good questions. For example, right now I'm looking at what appears to be a trail that will take us south, back up to the top of the rim. Is it Grandview Trail? If it is, then we need to turn here. If it's not, and we turn here anyway thinking that it is, we could end up in a lot of trouble. So what do we do?"

"Mitch, you're the guide. Please don't tell me you're lost!"

"McZen says that if you don't have a question, you don't have a clue; if you're not searching, you must be lost."

"Listen, Mitch, right now I couldn't care less what McZen says. Are we lost?"

"Charlie, your doubt is pushing you toward a panic attack. When you panic, you make bad decisions. You waste vital energy. Train your doubt, and start right now. First, how much water do we have – how long will it last us in a worst case?"

"We just filled the camelback," Charlie replied, "so we could probably go for several days if we're careful."

"Excellent! You've just trained your doubt. Instead of creating visions of two desiccated skeletons on the trail, your doubt now knows that we have enough water to make it back to the stream if we need to, and in a worst case we could refill our water containers there and hike back to the trail we came down in the first place. Take a look at the topo map here and tell me if you can approximate where we are, since you know where we started this morning."

Charlie scrutinized the map and made an educated guess as to their current location. "Not bad," Mitch responded, "certainly close enough for government work." Mitch pointed to a spot on the map and said, "This is the trailhead we need to locate to get up on Horseshoe Mesa, which is our stop for tonight. Look around and tell me if you see a structure that has this distinctive shape."

Charlie pointed to a large structure off to the right. "Very good, Charlie, that's terrific!"

"You mean I got it right?"

"No, actually you didn't. But you did point to something that looks a bit like Horseshoe Mesa. Look closer, though. It's not high enough – you see how Horseshoe Mesa towers above the surrounding terrain on the map here, but what you just pointed to is actually lower than the surrounding structures? How about that?" he continued, pointing to a plateau that was much more distant than what Charlie had been looking at.

Charlie shook his head. "Now I'm really confused."

"That's good," Mitch replied. "Now you can start to learn. You see, two minutes ago you were panicked. One minute ago you thought you knew the answer. Now you're willing to ask questions. You're learning to train your doubt." Mitch showed Charlie how to read the map correctly, and to feel confident when they had located the trail that would lead them out of the canyon. If nothing else, Charlie thought, this trip would give him a whole new appreciation for poets.

"There are three more things that can help you deal more effectively with worry," Mitch said. "The first is to follow the old advice to prepare for the worst, but expect the best. That's really what we've done on this journey. We are carrying all sorts of first aid supplies that we don't expect to use, but which could prove life-saving in certain circumstances. We don't let the fear of being bitten by a snake or breaking an ankle prevent us from enjoying the trip, but know that if it were to happen we have taken all possible steps to deal with it.

"The second is to reprogram your negative and pessimistic thinking patterns. When we get back, I'd like to give you the name of a woman who does hyper-hypnosis. It's an incredibly intense experience that can help you eradicate negative thought patterns and get out of emotional ruts.

"And the last thing is from another of McZen's poems. It says when you're afraid of the future you should concentrate on what you must do right now today, and when you're afraid of what's happening today, you should keep your vision on the future. It's a variation on McZen's *Be Today, See Tomorrow* paradox. The secret of happiness is to keep your attention in the present, but the key to success is to keep your vision in the future. How can you do them both at once? I don't know what the answer is for you, but I do know that to be both happy and successful, that's exactly what you must do."

***Be Today, See Tomorrow.* The secret of happiness is to keep your attention in the present, but the key to success is to keep your vision in the future.**

That night, their last in the canyon on this trip, the two men lay out under the stars. There was no moon, and Charlie couldn't remember ever having seen a more beautiful sky. He'd always believed that whenever he saw a shooting star, it portended good things. That night, the sky seemed to be alive with them. Charlie fell asleep with a smile.

CHAPTER FIVE

# Clean Up The Mess in Your Attic

When Mitch Matsui recommended hyper-hypnosis, Charlie had painted a mental image of an old woman named Madame Zelda in long purple robes with big, gold hoop earrings. Thus far, however, his introduction to Ronda Wellington had been utterly professional.

Wellington had sent him a pre-appointment survey which took the better part of a day to complete. It had asked him to catalog all of his fears and guilt feelings; the negative self-talk, self-images and self-beliefs that held him back; his worries, sources of stress, causes of procrastination, and self-sabotaging attitudes. If he'd ever had a negative thought, attitude, or emotion, Wellington's questionnaire wanted to know about it.

Her brochure had explained hyper-hypnosis as a full day series of hypnotherapy sessions, a sort of all-out assault on self-imposed limitations. "This is a massive intervention designed to interrupt self-defeating attitudes and behavior patterns, and through the art and science of Metaphorical Visualization to replace them with more useful mental tools," the brochure had concluded.

Now, walking into Wellington's office, Charlie saw what could have been the waiting room in any other professional business. The walls were adorned with paintings from K-Mart, and ancient additions of *People* magazine were scattered about on the end tables. There were no crystal balls, no magic charms, and no parrot squawking omens of dread and doom from a perch in the corner. Charlie checked in and the receptionist escorted him to a room at the back of the office suite. On the door was a sign that read:

QUIET PLEASE
MIRACLES WITHIN

Inside was a room much more like what Charlie had expected in the first place. It had thick, plush carpeting and was lighted only by a shaded lamp in the corner. There was no desk in the room, only a wooden captain's chair with a plain cushion on the seat and the most comfortable-looking black leather lounge chair Charlie had ever seen. The soft music of flutes and guitar suffused the room.

"Dr. Wellington will be with you in a moment. Why don't you make yourself comfortable and just relax," the receptionist said, motioning toward the easy chair. Charlie nestled into the chair as the door whispered shut behind the receptionist. The walls, he noticed, were covered with some sort of soundproofing material. His pre-appointment instructions had told Charlie to get a good night of sleep so he wouldn't fall asleep during the session, but in that environment it was still a struggle to stay alert as he waited.

He'd almost given in to sleep when the door opened again and a short, trim woman who appeared to be in her mid-fifties walked in. She was wearing a sharp blue business suit—no flowing purple robes! "Good morning, Charlie. I've spent so much time with your pre-appointment survey that I feel like I know you."

Charlie felt like a turtle on its back as he struggled to work his way out of the easy chair, but she motioned him to stay seated. "I'm Dr. Wellington, Ronda Wellington." She shook Charlie's hand, then took her place in the captain's chair, positioning it so Charlie could see her with only a slight twisting of his neck.

"You've read the brochure, so you know this will be a very intensive day." She pulled a clipboard from her attaché case and placed it on her lap. "Metaphorical Visualization is a revolutionary new method for rewriting some of the harmful scripts, negative self images, and destructive attitudes that can hold you back." Her smile and her manner exuded caring and competence, and Charlie felt an immediate bond of trust. "Basically, it's psychological judo. Rather than tackle the problems head on, we'll create visual and verbal metaphors—pictures of something else to represent the problems you would like to solve, and the tools you will need to solve them. Here's an example." She looked from Charlie down to her clipboard. "You enjoy automobile racing, don't you?"

Charlie nodded, recalling that was one of the special joys he'd indicated on the pre-appointment questionnaire.

"Imagine you have a busy day before you: projects to complete, meetings to attend, places to go, family and social activities, and so on. Instead of getting up in the morning and making a to-do list, you visualize your day as a Formula One racecourse. Picture any projects you're not looking forward to as tricky hairpin curves on that track – places where it's easy to spin out – and the fun stuff you see in your day ahead as long straightaways where you can jam your foot to the floor and really fly. Once you have the course all mapped out, picture yourself as a racecar, all fueled up and ready to go. Whenever you get bogged down during the day, recall that vision of the racecar named Charlie powering through the curves, and you tackle each task with renewed enthusiasm. That's how Metaphorical Visualization works."

"Sounds like fun," said Charlie.

"It is fun," replied Dr. Wellington. "In fact, it all started more than ten years ago when I was working with children to help them raise their self-esteem. Our most effective results came from these little mind games. And it turns out that it works even better with adults – perhaps because we want so deeply to reengage the spirit of play. We've adapted the technique to a whole range of conditions."

"Like helping people get unstuck?" Charlie asked.

"That's ninety percent of my business. Think of your mind as the attic in the house of your body. Like most attics everywhere, over time it becomes filled with all sorts of stuff – some of it useful, much of it not. Most of us don't take enough time to organize the attic. We need help. And that's what *The Janitor In Your Attic* is all about."

"The janitor in my attic? Sounds kind of silly!"

"Have any of the more serious things you've tried been very effective?"

"You've got me there." Charlie laughed. "Might as well have some fun working on it!"

"That's always been my attitude," said Dr. Wellington. "And you know what? Having fun turns out to be one of the most important predictors of success. The two others are faith and repetition. Now I can't make any guarantees, but I will tell you the more confident you are that this will help you, the more likely it is to work. Have you ever heard stories of people who, through the power of mental visualization, rid their bodies of cancer or brought about other seemingly miraculous cures?"

"Sure," said Charlie. "I've a friend who swears it was an essential factor in his recovery from leukemia."

**Metaphorical Visualization is like everything else in life. The more you practice it the better you will get at it, and the better your outcomes will be.**

"Well, it's the same with Metaphorical Visualization. The more certain you are that it will help you, the more certain it is to help you. And finally, like everything else in life, the more you practice it, the better you will get, and the better your outcomes will be. I'm going to give you some tapes to take home with you, which I hope you will listen to every day for the next several months. You really have to program this stuff in so that it's automatic."

Charlie frowned. "I read that in your brochure, and I'll have to say that I don't really feel comfortable with the notion of being programmed. It sounds too much like brainwashing."

"Well," Dr. Wellington replied, "every time you watch a TV commercial somone's trying to brainwash you, but sometimes a good washing can be a healthy thing! Especially when it's you doing the washing. Close your eyes for a minute now; visualize your own attic – your mind. Think of all the memories, the emotions, the thoughts, the facts and figures, the fears and doubts, the desires and ambitions, all that stuff that's up there fighting for your attention. Describe your attic for me, Charlie."

"Chaos. It's a mess."

"So let's use the power of metaphors to bring some order to the chaos. Some of the instincts that have been hardwired into your mind are obsolete. For example, the fight-or-flight reflex was very useful in protecting our caveman ancestors from sabertoothed tigers, but for most of the problems we face today fighting or running away is profoundly counterproductive. A great deal of self-sabotaging behavior is an instinctive reaction to ancient reflexes. To some extent, the hardware is obsolete, so you must consciously reprogram the software."

Charlie thought about his final meeting with Dick Dierdron. He'd wanted to punch him in the nose and then run away and hide. "I know what you mean," he smiled sheepishly.

"We're going to structure our day into four segments." Dr. Wellington held up four fingers, and as she listed each segment, she pushed one finger back down into her fist. "In session one, we'll go up into 'your attic' and begin to clean up the mess. In session two, we'll give you tools that will help you do a better job of effectively mastering your emotions. By then, you'll probably be hungry, so Rebecca will bring you a nice light and healthy lunch." She smiled and leaned forward, lightly poking Charlie in the ribs with her pen. "I don't want you falling asleep during the afternoon sessions!"

"In session three, we'll go through a routine that you should repeat every morning to help you program yourself for a great day. And finally, I'll give you an evening routine that will help you wind down and prepare yourself mentally and emotionally for the following day. I'll give you a CD that has both morning and evening tracks. You need to listen to these faithfully, every morning and evening for at least a month, until we're certain the new routines have been embedded in your subconscious mind."

Charlie leaned back in the chair and stretched his arms and legs. "Okay, I'm ready," he exclaimed.

"Before we get started, I need to introduce you to two important characters who are up there in your attic. You need to learn to recognize each of them, to know what they are doing, and learn how to make them work for you, and not against you. Now, I want you to close your eyes and relax." Dr. Wellington stood up and walked over to a panel on the wall, where she turned the music up slightly. Charlie did not see her walking back to her seat, only heard her voice floating back toward him across the room.

"The first character you need to visualize is nasty. He's mean and spiteful. He's a gremlin, a vandal. He's the one who is responsible for all of the negative self-talk, the sudden fears and worries, the self-imposed limitations, and all the other mental garbage that keeps you stuck in your rut. Can you picture him running around up there Charlie? Can you picture the little villain with a magic marker in his hand, painting graffiti on the walls of your mind? That's all negative self-talk is, you know. Mental graffiti.

Charlie instantly visualized an insidious little creature creeping around in his attic, marking up the walls with messages of negativity, pessimism, and despair.

"What's his name, Charlie?"

Without even thinking, Charlie was able to give the gremlin a name. "Gollum!"

"From Tolkien's *Hobbit* classics; how appropriate. Now imagine that you have a janitor up there, whose job it is to run around and clean up after Gollum. Someone who can help you clean up the mess and give you the tools to start building your attic into the nice place that you want it to be. Can you picture him?"

Charlie sat quietly for a while, breathing slowly and concentrating, then smiled and nodded his head. "What's his name?" Dr. Wellington asked.

Without hesitation, Charlie replied, "Spike! Spike was my high school football coach. He could handle any gremlin!"

"Very good, Charlie. Very good." She watched Charlie for a moment, his eyes still closed and deep in thought, then scanned through the notes on her clipboard.

"Now, Charlie, let's go up into the attic and straighten things out. Visualize yourself pulling down the ladder, and then crawling up into the attic of your mind. When you get up there, look around for a minute; visualize the mess, the chaos. Take a look at all the graffiti of negative self talk, the fog of confusion, the prison bars of fear and doubt, all the things you wrote about in your pre-appointment survey. All that mess is the work of your Gollum. You don't see Gollum right now, Charlie, because like most gremlins of his ilk, Gollum is a coward. As soon as you shine a light in him, he runs away. That's why it's so important to pay attention to what's going on up there in the attic at all times – to be mentally awake and alert and paying attention to your own thinking and feeling. Now, visualize Spike coming in to clean up the mess. Your only job is to relax, breathe slowly and deeply, and watch Spike go to work." Charlie smiled slightly and settled more deeply into the chair, then took a few deep breaths.

"Have you got the image of Spike in your mind?" Charlie nodded. "So the first thing he's going to do is clean out all the garbage that's littered around. There's a ton of garbage, isn't there, Charlie? You know what the computer guys say: garbage in, garbage out. For a lifetime, your mind has been letting all kinds of garbage come in. Oh, you weren't conscious of it at the time, but you let it in and it stayed." Dr. Wellington was scrutinizing Charlie. His eyes didn't open, but the smile had been replaced by a confused frown.

"Let's start with the easy stuff," she continued. "Almost every time you've watched television or gone to a movie, you've absorbed images of violence and negativity. Although you haven't been consciously aware of it, these images have slowly and insidiously shaped for you a vision of the world as a frightening and hostile place. Now, relax and breathe slowly; picture in your mind a garbage dumpster that's open at the top. Visualize Spike walking around with a broom and a dustbin, sweeping up all the images of hatred, violence, rejection, and death that you've seen during the thousands of hours you've spent in front of the television. Watch him dump those images into that garbage dumpster. Can you see him, Charlie, sweeping the place up?" Charlie nodded again.

"Concentrate, Charlie, fix that picture in your mind. Keep watching Spike, sweeping out those frightening and negative images." Charlie's brow furrowed as he struggled to keep the picture in his mind. Dr. Wellington continued. "Now, picture Spike driving up in a big forklift and hoisting that garbage dumpster full of negative images. Can you see it?" Charlie nodded. "Watch him drive the forklift over to a great big dumptruck, raise the lift as high as it will go, and drop all those negative images into a dumptruck. Can you see it, Charlie? Imagine that on the side of the truck the words are painted, 'Garbage Out.' Can you see that?"

Wellington watched Charlie breathe. "There's much work to be done up here, isn't there? Spike's just getting warmed up. Can you see him rolling up his sleeves like he really means business?" Charlie responded by simple squeezing his eyes more tightly shut as he struggled to keep the image in his mind. The music had become deeper and darker, with bassoons and bass replacing the flutes and guitar.

"Your attic is also full of mirrors. They are what creates your image of yourself, and it's often not a very flattering image. That's because most of the mirrors in *your* attic are funhouse mirrors! What you see when you look in them is not the real Charlie, but a twisted and distorted caricature. Those mirrors have to go! Can you see yourself walking up to one of those mirrors? Do you see how the glass waves and ripples, and throws back a cartoon image of you with stubby little legs and a neck like a giraffe?" Charlie smiled and snorted. He was drifting deeper into Dr. Wellington's game.

"That's the mirror Gollum put up to create a self-reflection of your business self. All those years at Logistics Precision, your colleagues thought you were so talented and capable, and you could only be astounded at how easily fooled they all were. Well, Charlie, they were seeing the real you and you were seeing the funhouse mirror image of you. And now, you're thinking about starting your own business. The real Charlie, the Charlie that everyone else sees, will succeed in that business. But the funhouse mirror Charlie would probably fail." Charlie shuddered slightly, then squirmed in the chair, squeezing his eyes more tightly shut.

"And here comes Spike, pulling a hammer out of his belt. Watch him, Charlie, as he yanks out the nails that are holding that funhouse mirror up, then rips it off the wall. It's heavy, so he struggles to manhandle it over to the dumpster. Watch him hoist it over the side, then listen to the shattering glass as it hits the bottom. Picture Spike hanging another mirror in its place, a normal mirror, and take a look. See yourself in that mirror, Charlie, the way everyone else sees you, dressed sharply in your business suit, a man who is obviously capable and trustworthy. That's the real Charlie McKeever, and that's the image you must permanently fix in your mind."

Dr. Wellington shifted slightly in her chair, never taking her eyes from Charlie's face. "Now watch Spike push his cart along to the next mirror. This one has a big bulge in the middle; it makes you look fat and ridiculous, like a soccer ball with toothpick arms and legs." Charlie laughed. "This is Charlie the parent as seen in Gollum's funhouse mirror. This is not the parent your children see – at least not most of the time," and here both Wellington and Charlie smiled, "but it's the picture Gollum wants you to see: spoiling your children rotten, doing a lousy job of disciplining, always at work when you should be at home – is this a familiar reflection?" Charlie nodded.

"Familiar, but not real. The real image is that you, like every other working person, are struggling to do your best to meet what often feels like an impossible load of demands, but the things you are doing right vastly outweigh the ones you're not doing right. So let's just have Spike rip down this mirror, and dump it – can you hear the glass break as it shatters at the bottom of the dumpster? – and put up a new mirror, one that reflects the real Charlie McKeever, who is a dedicated, loving and devoted husband and father."

Charlie's lip quivered as he thought about his family, and how badly he wanted to do the right thing for them. In that moment, he knew Dr. Wellington was right, that his image of himself as a worker and as a family man were not consistent with the real facts.

"There are many more funhouse mirrors to be removed, Charlie. That will be one of your assignments in the coming months. But if you look closely, you'll notice something else on the walls of your attic up there – lots of graffiti. That's the negative self talk, the doubt, the false beliefs that hold you back. You see, Charlie, Gollum is basically a lazy coward. He doesn't want to work hard, and he's afraid of change. So he paints the walls with lies about you and your abilities. You see those lies every day, and you begin to believe them."

Charlie's heart dropped, as though a sudden black cloud of dread had moved in and settled over him. Dr. Wellington's pre-appointment survey had asked him to make a list of all the negative self-talk he could identify; his list had gone on for three pages. Now the entire roster was playing back though his head, only it was as if someone else was talking to him, assuring him that he was not good enough, was not making it, would never make it. "This is ridiculous," that little voice chided. "Don't you have better things to do than lie in this chair all day playing mind games with this charlatan?'

"Gollum is painting on the walls up there again, isn't he?" Dr. Wellington asked. Charlie nodded. "That's a good sign. He's feeling threatened; you're loosening his control, and that scares him beyond imagination. And here comes Spike, just in time."

Charlie clamped his eyes shut even tighter, struggling to bring back the image of Spike. Dr. Wellington continued, "Spike is pushing a utility cart full of paint cans and brushes. Pay attention Charlie. He's prying the lid off of a can of paint and stirring it up. Now watch him go up to each piece of graffiti, all that negative self talk, all those lies that Gollum keeps repeating in your head, and cover them up with clean white paint. The words 'You're a loser' painted out – gone. And from the bottom of his cart, Spike pulls out a beautiful little needlepoint and hangs it on the wall where the graffiti was before. It says, 'I Am a Winner and Winners Don't Quit.' Can you read it Charlie?"

At the corner of awareness, Charlie noticed a flute floating above the bassoons as Wellington spoke again. "You made the most important step before you ever came to my office, Charlie, and that was when you wrote down your repertoire of negative self talk. Now you recognize it for what it is, and every time it comes up you can holler for Spike to paint it out and replace it with something that's positive and true. After a while, once Spike is embedded in your mind as deeply as Gollum is now, this process will become automatic. And the more you do it, the easier it will get. There's a lot more graffiti to be cleaned up in the following months, but for now you and Spike need to do something about the weeds of doubt."

Charlie wasn't sure where he was on the continuum between wakefulness and sleep as he peered down a long dark hallway sided by walls covered with graffiti, and gave a start when Wellington spoke again. "In the pre-appointment survey, you described your dream of the ideal future. It's a beautiful dream: building a business that creates jobs and touches many lives in a positive way; spending your days doing work you love to do; building your dream house out in the country. Frankly, Charlie, it's a dream you can make happen, and it's a dream you deserve to enjoy seeing happen."

Dr. Wellington looked closely to gauge the impact of her words, but Charlie showed no change in expression. "I want you to picture that dream now Charlie, see your ideal future as a beautiful garden. Imagine the most beautiful place you have ever seen. On the canvas of your mind, paint a place that is alive with flowers and bushes, plants and trees. See the flowers in a riot of red, pink, orange and blue, and the trees and bushes in all their greens and yellows and browns, swaying in a soft breeze. Let each tree and bush, every flower, represent a goal you have accomplished. Walk through your garden. Listen to the little brook that babbles underneath the footbridge that leads into it. That's the future you deserve Charlie. A place of breath-taking splendor and peace."

Dr. Wellington noted the slight smile now on Charlie's face, and that he was breathing more slowly and deeply. She sat quietly for several minutes, allowing him to savor the image. Then she took a deep breath and continued. "That picture, that garden, is your certainty. It's your destiny – your memory of the future. But you can't always see it so clearly, can you? It's as if some days your garden has been choked over by weeds, and they grow so fast that pretty soon they're all you can see. Those weeds are your doubts: doubts about yourself, about your ideas, about other people, doubts about money – your doubts are the weeds choking the garden. While you're out there in the future building your beautiful garden – your memory of the future – your little gremlin, Gollum, is up in the attic planting seeds of doubt. And of course, everyone knows that weeds grow much more quickly than flowers do. Unless you take immediate action to eradicate those doubts, they can choke out the flowers before they ever have a chance to establish themselves."

As Charlie visualized the garden of his dream future being choked over by weeds, he felt an infinite sadness, an emptiness he had not experienced since his beloved boyhood dog was hit by a car. He felt helpless and paralyzed as he watched a jungle of weeds sprouting, creeping, and blossoming throughout his garden. Then, as each one opened its hideous head to the sun, it spewed out a horde of new doubts, more terrifying and paralyzing than their progenitors had been. At that moment, Charlie felt the emptiness of a farmer watching his crop being devastated by locusts, or of a businessman watching his factory burning to the ground in a fire. Dr. Wellington could see his teeth grinding as impotent rage welled up in his heart.

Wellington nodded to herself. "I want you to picture yourself on this side of that footbridge looking into your garden. You can only catch glimpses of the garden through the forest of weeds, and the bridge itself is choked to a complete close. Can you see that Charlie?"

Charlie nodded almost imperceptibly. "You feel helpless, don't you? Helpless and furious." Charlie felt again the emptiness he'd experienced at the funeral of his little dog. "Now focus in more closely on the image of you. Notice that you're wearing work clothes: you've got on denim coveralls, a red flannel shirt, and heavy work boots. Can you see that?" Charlie nodded. "Zoom in on your head and notice that you're wearing industrial eyeglasses and ear protection. Can you see it?" Charlie nodded again. "Look again, Charlie. That image must be crystal clear in your mind: you in your work clothes – your battle gear so to speak – standing at the foot of the bridge. Can you see yourself there?" Charlie took a deep breath and nodded again.

"Take a closer look at your face, Charlie. Have you ever seen such a look of determination? Your jaw is set firmly, your eyes are clear and resolved. You are the hero, Charlie, who will not give up the quest without one last gallant fight." Dr. Wellington noticed Charlie's jaw set as his real face mirrored the picture in his mind. "You are the hero, but there's one thing missing, isn't there? King Arthur had his sword, Joan of Arc had her lance. You need a weapon, don't you? Look down at your hands, Charlie, and take a look at what you're holding. It is a giant…" she paused for what seemed an eternity as Charlie's fingers clenched to grasp his imaginary weapon "…weedwhacker!" A huge smile lit up Charlie's face. At that moment, his expression reminded Dr. Wellington of her teenage son slaughtering evil aliens down at the video arcade. "Watch yourself pull the starter, and hear it roar into action. What you have in your hands is a Sears best-quality industrial-strength weedwhacker. And you're a hero on a mission. Your mission, Charlie, is to save the garden of your future dreams from those weeds of doubt. Rev up your weedwhacker, Charlie, and start walking across the bridge chopping down every weed into a shredded, mangled stump."

By now, Charlie was totally absorbed in the game. Dr. Wellington smiled and leaned back in her chair as Charlie's arms lurched back and forth, hewing down the imaginary villains on the bridge. "Keep going, Charlie! Keep going! Go save the rosebushes. Rescue the birdbath. Clear out the path to the gazebo!" She sat silently for a few minutes as Charlie continued his assault on the barbarian weeds. At length, she spoke again: "Oh, good, here comes Spike. He's pushing a great big wheelbarrow and has a couple of rakes. It's time to set aside the weedwhacker and get rid of the carnage. Do you see yourself and Spike raking up all those dead weeds and throwing them in the wheelbarrow?" Charlie nodded. "Good. Once the wheelbarrow is full, Spike will take them out to be burned. And while he does that, you will spread weed killer all around the garden. That will keep the weeds from coming back for a while. But I must warn you, weeds of doubt are not like ordinary weeds. They're tougher and more resilient. But if you spend a little time weeding the garden of your future dreams every day, it will stay beautiful."

Charlie sighed deeply, in the manner of someone who has just completed a tough and challenging task. "Now, picture yourself again. You're a mess, but a happy mess. There's dirt all over your face, except for two big white circles where your safety glasses were. Your clothes are filthy, and your boots are caked with mud. But there's a huge smile on your face. Now, just walk around your garden for a bit. It's beautiful again, isn't it? And off in the distance, up on a small hill, your dream house faces out over the pond. Luxuriate in this vision, Charlie. You've worked hard, and you've earned it."

Dr. Wellington was quiet for a long time, allowing Charlie to revel in the dream. She didn't speak again until she noticed him starting to fidget. "There's one more job we have to do, Charlie, and I've saved the most difficult and dangerous job for last. When you were preparing yourself for this visit, I had you make a list of the fears you see holding yourself back. It was quite a list, Charlie, an ugly list. Gollum has taken all of those fears, any one of which might have been only a little obstacle, a small stone you could easily step over, and amalgamated them into a huge rock of fear. I want you to picture that rock now, Charlie. Gollum has taken all of your fears – fears of failure, rejection, bankruptcy, humiliation, commitment, and all the others, and cemented them together into a massive stone of dread. Visualize this boulder now, Charlie – see in your mind the massive weight of your fears, and the jagged edges that cause you so much pain. It's much too big to move, because by the time Gollum has added all of your fears, it's not just a boulder; it's a small mountain. What are we going to do with this huge rock of fear, Charlie?"

Charlie shook his head and shrugged. In his mind, he was seeing a miniature version of El Capitan at Yosemite: massive and immoveable.

**Your subconscious mind will take all of your little fears and amalgamate them together into a massive stone of dread, so you need to explode it into smaller pieces so that you can deal with them one by one.**

"Well," continued Dr. Wellington, "like any other huge undertaking, we're just going to have to break it into smaller parts." A sudden confusion set into Charlie's features so she explained. "We're going to blow that rock up, Charlie, blast it to smithereens! For this job, however, Spike needs professional help. Picture a road leading up to that big rock of fear. You and Spike are standing at the end of the road, in the shadow of the rock, and you're waiting."

This was always Dr. Wellington's favorite part. It was why she called Metaphorical Visualization her "magical science." At some point during every successful session, the process transcended science and became something more mystical – something magic. That was happening now. She and Charlie were synchronizing. She felt herself being guided by some greater awareness to the images, the metaphors, that would be most effective in helping Charlie get unstuck. It was the hardest work she would ever do; she never scheduled appointments the day after a hyper-hypnosis session because she was physically, emotionally, and spiritually exhausted. But right now, she was in that exalted state of flow where the world outside disappears, time stands still. If she was successful, she knew that for the rest of his life Charlie would consider this day to have been a dramatic turning point. There was a cataclysmic struggle being fought on an emotional and a spiritual plane, and she could not afford to lose. By the end of the day, she and Charlie, linked together in synchronous flow, had to subjugate Gollum and take away from him the weapons he used to terrify Charlie into a state of passive submission.

"You and Spike are looking at this hideous boulder, wondering how you can ever get it out of the way, when you hear a rumbling noise headed down the road in your direction. You look back, and see a column of dust rising in the distance. Watch it as it gets closer, and the noise becomes louder and more distinct. Now you see it's a column of trucks. They're drab green with big white stars, so you know it's a military battalion. Now Spike tells you it's the demolition team he's called for. They're going to blow up the rock, and haul out the pieces."

Dr. Wellington paused to allow Charlie to paint the mental image, then went on. "The column pulls to a stop. A couple of Humvees at the front, and then a whole line of bulldozers and dumptrucks. A man jumps out of the leading vehicle. He looks like someone you've seen before. He's got a red bandanna wrapped around his head, and he's not wearing a shirt so you can see he's got huge muscles."

Charlie mouthed the world, "Rambo."

"Actually, you've just met Spike's friend Ramrock. He's the demolition expert. Now you see men piling out of Jeeps and trucks, and they're all carrying equipment of some sort. Watch them, Charlie, as they go up to your big rock of fear and begin drilling holes – can you hear the jackhammers? – and then stuffing them full of explosives. It's a huge rock, so this is going to take a while." Dr. Wellington paused for a moment, as Charlie visualized Ramrock's demolition team swarming over his rock of fear like ants on a candy bar.

"Now, watch Ramrock going around and carefully inspecting each and every charge. He's checking the wiring to make sure it's properly connected, and then running it back to the detonator. Can you see that?" Charlie nodded. "Now they've lined up all the dumptrucks to form a protective shield, and you and Spike are huddled down behind a great big wheel. You hear Ramrock hollering for everyone to get down, and look up just in time to see him pushing the plunger of the detonator. Instantly, it seems that you've been plunged into the pit of hell. There is a searing flash of light and heat, followed immediately by the loudest explosion you've ever heard. Then the rocks start falling. Can you see yourself huddling under the truck to get out of the way?" Charlie nodded.

"When the dust finally clears, you crawl out from under the truck. The big, ugly rock of fear is gone. Instead, the ground is littered with all the rocks that represent each individual fear. Watch yourself, Charlie, as you walk over and pick up the rock which represents your fear of humiliation. It's heavy, but by itself, it's manageable. Watch yourself heave it up over the side of one of Ramrock's dumptrucks. Can you see that?" Charlie nodded. "Good. Now, just sit back and relax and watch Ramrock's team go to work. There are bulldozers everywhere, pushing the rocks into piles, and then shoveling them into the dumptucks." She paused as Charlie visualized this. "When all the rocks have been cleaned up, Ramrock says goodbye and leads his crew back down the road where they came from. You and Spike turn around, and there in the distance is your dream, your memory of the future, and the rock of fear no longer stands in your way.

"It's a beautiful, sunny day and you are experiencing a freedom you've not felt in a long time – freedom from fear. Your attic is clean and organized, and we've taken all of the garbage out: all the funhouse mirrors, the graffiti on the walls, the weeds of doubt, the rocks of fear, it's all gone. I'm going to leave for a while now Charlie, and let you enjoy your peace and your freedom. When you're ready, get up and move around a little bit. Drink a glass of water. When I come back, we'll begin our second session, where we build the infrastructure and give you the tools that will assure your success at achieving your memory of the future."

Charlie was still resting in the chair when Dr. Wellington returned. She touched him lightly on the shoulder, and then resumed her seat in the captains chair. "How are you doing?"

Charlie laughed. "I think I have a headache from when Ramrock demolished that rock."

"I'm not surprised," said Dr. Wellington. "I could feel the shock wave all the way across the room!"

They both laughed, then sat in silence for a moment before Dr. Wellington asked Charlie if he was ready to continue. He nodded, closed his eyes, and stretched back into the chair. "Picture yourself back at the entry to the attic," she instructed. "See yourself pulling down the ladder again and climbing up into the attic of your mind. Take a look around and enjoy it, Charlie, because you might not ever see your attic this clean again."

Charlie smiled as his attention drifted inward. At that moment, it almost seemed he could smell the fresh white paint and see his image reflected off of the sparkling linoleum floors. "For this next session," Dr. Wellington continued, "we're going to be doing some heavy construction. Working in your attic is a lot like refurbishing an old house – it's a project that never ends. But in this session, we're going to install some equipment and machinery that will help you keep Gollum under control, and stay focused on your memories of the future.

"The first step is to give you a way to keep your attic organized. Every day, you are faced with a barrage of new information, old memories, thoughts and emotions, and it can all be overwhelming at times. So what we're going to do is visualize Spike constructing a massive set of shelving in the warehouse section of the attic. It's essential that you visualize this very clearly now, so you can come back to it quickly later. Imagine Spike putting up steel shelves, row after row of them, in your mental warehouse. Can you see him working as he drags the shelves in, hear the pounding as he fixes each one in place?" Charlie smiled. "Good. You just keep watching Spike work. Let me know with a small nod of your head when Spike is done, and the entire warehouse is fitted out with shelving from one end to another."

Dr. Wellington watched patiently until Charlie gave a small nod of his head. "Now, Charlie, imagine Spike carrying in boxes and putting them on the shelves. The boxes are of all different sizes and many colors – some are even an unusual shape. Watch him put the boxes neatly up on the shelves. He's putting some of them up on the shelves labeled 'Emotions,' some of them go on the shelves labeled

'Names to Remember,' others are going on the shelves labeled 'Facts' and 'Figures.' On and on he goes, down the rows of shelving, and as he does he's sorting out all the knowledge, the emotions, the thoughts, everything that goes on in your head. Keep watching him load boxes as I talk." Charlie nodded again, very slightly.

"Here's how you're going to use those shelves, you and Spike. Every time you learn something new, you'll take a second to visualize Spike putting that box of information in the proper place on the shelves. Likewise, every time you meet a new person, you'll close your eyes for just a second to visualize Spike putting a box with that person's name and image in the right place on the shelves. Any time you have a hard time remembering something or someone, rather than fighting to dig up the name by yourself, you will simply visualize Spike going back through the shelves and bringing you the right box. You'll be surprised, but the more you practice the more you'll find that this indirect approach actually works better."

Charlie watched Spike struggle to hoist a particularly large box onto the shelves. Wellington went on. "You know how you can become confused when you get fatigued late in the day?" Charlie nodded. "Again, don't fight it. Rather take a few minutes to sit quietly with your eyes closed and look up in the attic. What you'll see is that your warehouse looks like it's been shaken by a minor earthquake and there are boxes everywhere. Don't try to think it through at this point, simply watch Spike going up and down the rows of shelves, picking up boxes and putting them back in their proper place. Very shortly, you'll feel like you are back in control." Charlie watched Spike work, and noticed that the music had given way to a single guitar. "Okay," Wellington said, "take one last look back at the warehouse. Are all the boxes up off the floor and on the shelves?" Charlie nodded with a slight smile. *If only it would be so easy,* he heard a small voice inside his head say, and then another voice replied, it can be.

"The next thing Spike needs to do is install fire alarm and sprinkler systems. Often, your emotions act the same way a fire does in a building. They build up slowly and covertly, creating stress and emotional tension. Then, seemingly without warning, they erupt into a full blown temper tantrum, panic attack, or stress-out. The trick is to see it coming and then have a system to douse the flames before they rage out of control and cause you to do something or say something you'll regret later. So right now, picture Spike going around putting up smoke detectors throughout the attic. He's putting up red detectors for anger, purple detectors for stress, and yellow detectors for fear. If you can fix these images solidly in your subconscious mind, they'll go off when your emotional temperature starts to rise. If you're paying attention, you'll hear them, take a deep breath, and calm back down. For the times when you don't catch it in time, we'll also need a back-up system to put out the flames."

**Your emotions can act the same way a fire does in a building. They build up slowly and covertly, creating stress and emotional tension. Then, seemingly without warning, they erupt into a full blown temper tantrum, panic attack, or stress-out.**

As Wellington spoke, Charlie noticed how that creating a mental image of Spike working was coming much more easily. "Here comes Spike again, and this time he's pushing a cart loaded with PVC piping. This is for your emotional fire sprinkler system. As you watch him setting up his ladder and begin hanging these pipes from the ceiling, and then installing the sprinkler heads in them, think of the situations where you will want this sprinkler system to go off before your emotional flames get out of control. When a building is burning down, it's too late to install a sprinkler system. Likewise, the more you can anticipate the frightening, angering, and stressful situations that might send you off the handle, the more effectively your subconscious mind will activate this system in time to prevent a blow-out. Finally, picture Spike installing a mammoth exhaust fan at one end of the building. When your sprinkler system goes off to put out a fire, there's likely to be a lot of smoke in the aftermath. That makes it hard to see reality effectively. If you close your eyes for a moment, breathe deeply, and visualize this giant exhaust fan blowing away the smoke of anger, stress, and panic, you'll recover much more quickly."

Wellington waited longer than usual, seeing that Charlie was deeply engrossed in this mental construction project. "Before you leave today, I'm going to give you a map of your newly outfitted attic. Until you have it totally memorized, you'll want to spend some time every day mentally walking through this map, and visualizing all the new equipment that's been installed. Like the auxiliary powered generator, which is our next item. We all have moments when we run out of energy. In your pre-appointment survey, you mentioned that this often happens to you in mid-afternoon. Now, instead of running out for a cup of coffee and a candy bar, you can just visualize this emergency power generator kicking in to give you the boost you need until your primary system kicks in again. In today's afternoon sessions, I'll show you how to keep it charged and ready; for now it's only important that you visualize this big generator being installed in as much detail as possible, and that you believe it will start up any time your energy level starts to fade."

Charlie thought about the inevitable slump that followed his afternoon candy bar and cup of coffee, and from the shadows of his mind heard Gollum wail that he could never go a day without them. "While we're in the heavy equipment zone," Wellington said, "there are still a few more things to do. First, let's check out the furnace of desire – the old fire in the belly. Can you see it there, big and brooding? Looking like something that's been misplaced from a steel foundry? We all have a furnace like that, but unfortunately in most people it's grown stone cold. Can you feel the warmth of your furnace as we get closer? The day you can visualize that furnace and actually break out in a sweat is the day you become unstoppable. Now, visualize that beside the furnace door is a big pile of logs; logs of ambition. In the afternoon session, I'm going to show you how to make daily rounds through your attic. One of the things you'll do is toss another log of ambition into the furnace of desire every time you pass by. As you visualize that furnace becoming hotter and hotter, you will become more and more determined to succeed."

The music was still soft and soothing, but Charlie noticed that a distant french horn gave it a new sense of urgency as Wellington spoke again. "As you go through the workbook and tapes I'm going to give you, you'll undoubtedly design some new heavy equipment of your own. But before we go up to the control center, let's install one of my favorite pieces of industrial machinery – the electromagnet of universal awareness. Picture in your mind a giant magnet. It's U-shaped, with wire coils wrapped around it, and it's connected to a control panel with a keyboard. At any time, whatever you most need, type your need as clearly and explicitly as possible into this keyboard. Are you visualizing a keyboard with a screen set in the middle of the control panel? Once you've entered what you need, visualize a big power switch and see yourself turning it in. The electromagnet will then begin to send out the signals that will attract the help, the money, and whatever else you need and have programmed into the control panel. It's especially helpful, when you get discouraged, to remember that electromagnetic waves are invisible. The magnet may be pulling something in your direction which you can't yet see, but will surely come to you so long as you don't quit."

In his mind, Charlie stood dwarfed at the base of the electromagnet, and could hear it thrumming its message out to the universe. "One more stop, Charlie, and it's the most important one: the control center. Imagine the thinking part of your brain as a magnificent computer. This afternoon, I'll show you how to program it with positive and affirming screen savers, but for now let's visualize Spike upgrading the memory and central processing unit. Imagine him installing new circuits and bigger disk drives in your brain. It won't happen immediately, of course, but the more often you visualize your mental hardware being upgraded, the more effectively your mind will work." Charlie nodded and flexed his fingers. "Now imagine you've entered the communications center. Up here, we need to install two vital pieces of equipment. First is a highly sensitive satellite dish to bring in signals from all over the universe. You know, many of the ancient mystics believed that we are all profoundly connected in the web of life. Modern research into the nature of prayer suggests they weren't far wrong. The simple act of someone thinking a positive thought about you can give you strength and courage, even if they are far away. Even if you're not consciously paying attention, embedding this satellite dish in your subconscious will help you collect healthy and positive emanations from all around you. Equally important is the broadcast antenna. Picture something that looks like a short wave radio set. Anytime you find yourself hurting or in need of something, simply pick up the microphone and broadcast your plea – or if you prefer, your prayer – out into the universe, and believe that it will be guided to the person most able to help you."

Charlie nodded. Just the other day he'd been thinking of Cheryl von Noyes, and within minutes she'd called his cell phone. "Just two more stops, but both of them are vitally important. First is your future scope. Imagine something that looks a lot like a periscope. Any time you feel overwhelmed by the daily press of events and lose sight of your ultimate goal, stop and relax for a moment. Imagine yourself raising this scope way up high, above the chaos that seems to swirl all about you. Point it in the direction of your memory of the future, and the vision will help you keep your current circumstances in a better perspective."

**The simple act of someone thinking a positive thought about you can give you strength and courage, even if they are far away.**

An image of an airliner breaking out above the cloud layer popped into Charlie's mind, an image in which the view went on to an infinite horizon. "Finally," Wellington said, "let's visit your navigation center. This contains two very important devices. First is a compass, keeping you pointed in the direction of that memory of the future. Any time your intuition tells you that you're getting off track, take a moment to visualize this compass. Your subconscious wisdom will help guide you back in the right direction. And last but not least, picture a big flywheel, just like the flywheel on the engine of a car, spinning around to keep your momentum going. Any time you feel yourself bogging down, losing momentum, visualize this flywheel, spinning 'round and 'round, keeping you going during the times that Gollum would rather you give up."

Before concluding the morning session, Wellington took Charlie on a grand tour of his newly cleaned and remodeled attic. Together, they walked through the garden of his future dreams, inspected the walls to make sure that Gollum hadn't put up any new graffiti, polished the new self-image mirrors, and picked up the last few rock fragments from the boulder of fear that Ramrock and his crew had exploded. Then they double-checked all the new equipment they'd installed.

After lunch, Dr. Wellington gave Charlie mental routines for getting started in the morning, and for ending each day. He visualized Spike going through his attic, stoking up the furnace of desire, programming positive and affirming screen savers into his mental PC, reorganizing the boxes on the utility shelving, cleaning up the walls and polishing the mirrors. Charlie came up with some of his own metaphorical visualizations, including a first aid kit for hurt feelings and having Spike put up roadblocks on all the detours – the fears and doubts – that Gollum tried to place on the road leading to his dreams of the future.

At the end of the day, Wellington gave him several workbooks and a set of audiotapes. And a hug. "You're a winner, Charlie. The world really needs to have your dreams come true. Don't ever let Gollum get the upper hand, not ever again."

As Charlie walked to his car that evening, he saw another memory of the future. His organization would become a vehicle by which Dr. Wellington could share the art and science of Metaphorical Visualization with millions of others. Charlie heard Gollum sniggering, then visualized Spike grabbing the little vandal by the scruff of the neck and stuffing him into one of the little cages that Pam used to take their animals to the vet. "You stay in there for a while," Spike said. "I'll let you out when you learn how to behave yourself." Charlie sat behind the wheel and imagined himself getting ready for a big formula one race tomorrow. He was going to enjoy using Metaphorical Visualization!

CHAPTER SIX

# MAKE FEAR YOUR ALLY AND ADVERSITY YOUR TEACHER

After leaving Dr. Wellington, Charlie had gone back home and worked on his *Empowerment Pyramid Workbook.* Incorporating many of the insights he'd learned from his trip to the Grand Canyon with Mitch Matsui and in his hyper-hypnosis session with Dr. Wellington, he was able to achieve a level of clarity previously inaccessible to him. Now, on one piece of paper, he had distilled a sense of purpose and direction that could serve as a guide for refining his own memories of the future. He picked it up and read it again.

The first block of the Empowerment Pyramid – IDENTITY – had yielded the biggest surprise. His real identity was totally incompatible with being a business consultant and corporate bureaucrat. In fact, for as long as he pursued that path, he was destined to eventual failure. He now realized that his authentic identity was much more as a crusader and as an entrepreneur. He shuddered to realize how badly he had distorted the "real him" to make it fit inside a cubicle at LPI.

The day he was working on his mission statement to include in the Pyramid's second block – MISSION – Charlie happened to read a cover article in *Fortune* magazine called "Finished at 40." It was about people just like him who, as they approached what should have been their peak earning years, had been let go by their companies. Ironically, Charlie found himself feeling distinctly unsympathetic to the complaints of people worried about their big houses and fancy cars, their six-figure paychecks, and their 401(k) plans. If they would spend less time whining about the temporary reduction they might have to make in their standard of living and spend more time figuring out how they could make a real contribution, they'd be much happier, he found himself thinking. In the long run, they'd probably be a lot richer to boot! These people need a support group, Charlie thought, an organized program that could teach them the skills and give them the courage to let go of the past, to stop worrying about money and status, and to think big, dream big, and achieve big. There was, Charlie knew, no such support group. Was it possible, he wondered, to build a successful business by creating programs of this type? It would certainly be compatible with his newly discovered sense of identity. He started writing, and after several drafts, had a mission statement with a solid ring of authenticity:

> *My mission is to build a worldwide organization that gives people tools and resources that will help them create meaning and also create wealth in their lives and in the lives of others.*

Charlie had known he was on the right track when he shared it with Pam and she smiled and gave him a big hug. "Create the meaning and the wealth will create itself," she'd said, with a lot more confidence than Charlie felt at the time. But the mission excited him and he spent many subsequent hours working on a vision statement to implement it:

> *What would the world look like if I were becoming the person I am truly meant to be, and enthusiastically pursuing my real mission in life?*

Just as Dr. Wellington had said it would, every time he tried to create a mental picture of his vision for the ideal future, the weeds of doubt began to cover it up. Using his new "weedwhacker" was the first real use he put to the tools she'd given him, and he was surprised at how effective it was. The images had begun to flow more and more smoothly, one into another. In his mind, he saw a whole catalog with the types of products that had been so helpful to him in recent weeks – like *The Janitor in Your Attic* and the *Empowerment Pyramid Workbook*. Charlie envisioned groups of people meeting every week, all across the country, to support and encourage each other – and periodically, everyone coming together at huge conventions. Naturally, with his technical background at LPI, he also saw a big role for Internet-based programs.

Soon, the vision was growing too fast for the weeds to keep up with it. Charlie saw himself leading small groups of inward-explorers into great places like the Grand Canyon, in much the same way Mitch Matsui had led him several months earlier. Cross country bike rides, youth programs, entrepreneurship festivals, summer success camps – Charlie smiled to think that Spike would have to add an additional aisle of shelving in the attic just to hold all the new boxes full of ideas. The vision was beginning to be a bit overwhelming, but the immediate action steps were becoming crystal clear. Charlie would need help, and he would need money.

So now, he found himself standing outside the door of his bank. Earlier in the day, he'd signed a licensing agreement with Dr. Wellington to develop a family of products built around *The Janitor in Your Attic* theme, and had incorporated his company as The Courage Place, Inc. at his attorney's office. And several minutes ago, he had signed the biggest loan he'd ever taken out, pledging the entirety of his personal assets as collateral. Suddenly, he felt like someone who had just started down a very steep mountain on a pair of skis. There was no stopping, there was no turning back. It was exhilarating. It was terrifying.

Charlie had no more appointments that day, the sun was shining, and Pam had taken the kids to a symphony rehearsal to teach them culture – after bribing them with a promise of pizza and ice cream afterwards – so he decided to take a walk. Feeling pulled to his right, he headed down the street. After several blocks, he felt a tug toward the left, so he followed it. After a few more turns, he realized his feet were leading him towards the Downtown Gym, run by his old friend Nick Amatuzzo.

Nick had been a champion professional fighter. He'd also been an alcoholic and a drug addict. He'd known both the winning side and the losing sides of life. For the past twenty years, he'd put his heart and soul into the Downtown Gym. It had started as a haven for troubled boys whose only alternative might have been life with the gangs, but later evolved into one of the city's most popular recreation and fitness clubs. Though he was now back on the winning side of life, Nick never forgot the lessons he learned from his days of trouble, and never gave up on his commitment to the kids.

As he rounded the corner, Charlie saw the big sign over the gym's front window – and the message that had drawn him there in the first place, years ago:

## Make Fear Your Ally<br>Make Adversity Your Teacher

Charlie saw Nick prowling through the weight room talking with clients and making sure everything was just right. He knew he could expect a warm welcome. Not only were they good friends, but he and Pam had been among the gym's most generous supporters in its early days. Pam even picked Nick's kids up after school and gave them rides to the gym.

Charlie waited by the counter, watching Nick make his way through the weight room. He didn't recognize many of the people working out, but Nick seemed to know everyone. He stopped for a bit longer at the bench press station, yelling encouragement at a powerfully-built young man who was straining to lift a barbell that Charlie guessed to weigh about as much as a Volkswagen. A final heave pushed the bar to a position above its resting cradle, where Nick and another spotter guided it home. The young man sat up and Charlie recognized Bill Duffey, one of the young men that

Pam used to pick up after school. Duffey was one of Nick's success stories; he'd earned a degree from Saint Johns and now worked as a loan officer for the biggest bank in town – the bank to which Charlie had just mortgaged all of his earthly possessions.

Eventually, Nick saw Charlie and walked over. "You're getting a little pudgy, there, marshmallow," he kidded, poking Charlie in the ribs. "Where's your gear? There's an exercise bike out there with your name on it. You know what old Teddy R. said, that it's better to wear out than it is to rust out."

"Not today, Nick. I'll come in over the weekend – promise. But if you've got some time, I actually have something serious I'd like to talk with you about."

Nick looked suddenly concerned. "Everything okay at home, Charlie, with Pam and the kids?"

"Yeah, Nick, everything's fine. It's really more about work. I got fired, you know. I don't work at LPI anymore."

"Gee, I hadn't heard that. How long ago?"

"Six weeks."

"Hmph." Nick scratched a bristly cheek and looked down at the floor. "Back in the workforce, huh? That's what happened to most of the guys here right now."

"Really?" Charlie guessed there were at least fifty people working out in the weight room and on the exercise machines beyond.

"Sure. Look at the clock." Charlie checked the wall behind the counter. It was 3:15 in the afternoon. "A year, two years ago, most of these guys were sitting behind desks at some company downtown. Then one day, *Bang!*" Nick smashed his right fist into his left palm to emphasize the point, "they get a pink slip and they're back in the workforce."

Charlie shook his head. "You mean they're *out of* the workforce, don't you?"

Nick laughed. "Heck, no, I don't. What most of those guys were doing wasn't really work. They were sitting in boring meetings, writing memos, talking on the phone. Now, they're coming face-to-face with the fact that no one's gonna pay 'em to do that anymore. They're gonna have to start making something that someone else wants and then sell it to them at a profit, or they're gonna starve."

Nick looked into the weight room and shook his head. "Look at 'em, Charlie, all pumped up and strutting around like Greek gods. And you know what? Inside, most of 'em are scared to death."

Now Charlie laughed. "So am I, Nick. Getting thrown out of the old comfortable workplace and into the tough new workforce is the most terrifying thing I've ever been through."

Nick put an arm around Charlie's shoulders and started walking back around the reception counter toward his office. Even though it had been over twenty years since Nick had been in the ring, he was still hard as stainless steel. Charlie guessed that facing Nick in the ring would still be far more terrifying than entering into a competitive marketplace.

One whole wall of Nick's office was lined with pictures of famous fighters. Most of them were pictured shaking hands with, or shaking a fist at, Nick. It was a who's-who of the ring: Dempsey, Ali, Hagler, both Sugar Rays, Forman and Fraser, and many others Charlie didn't recognize. In the place of honor behind Nick's desk, however, were pictures of men much less famous, but who owned the lion's share of Nick's heart: the boys he'd helped raise from juvenile delinquency to adult responsibility. Without asking Charlie whether he wanted one, Nick poured both men a cup of coffee as they sat at his small conference table. "Nick, you're getting soft in your old age," Charlie chided. "Real chairs?" In the early days, Nick's office had been outfitted like a boxing ring, with turnbuckles in all the corners and nothing to sit on but the stubby little stools that fighters rested on between rounds.

"Had to do it for the yuppies," Nick replied. "We'd give 'em the grand tour of the place and they'd be ready to sign up. Then we'd bring them back here and have 'em sit on a stool, and they'd get cold feet, wanna go home and think about it for a while. Before long, we'd find out they'd signed up at the Pink Slipper Boutique." Nick was referring to his cross-town competitor, which catered to a softer crowd. "So what's on your mind, Charlie?"

Charlie sipped Nick's industrial strength coffee and began. "I've decided to start my own business, Nick. You know Cheryl von Noyes, don't you?" Nick nodded. "She says that the letters J-O-B stand for jilted, obsolete, and broke. I don't ever want to be in that position again, so I'm going to take charge of my own destiny. I incorporated it today. It's called The Courage Place. I'm still working on the details, but it's going to be a membership organization that's part support group, part training center, and part adventure team."

"That's terrific, Charlie!" Nick beamed. "Heck, I bet we could walk out to the exercise room right now and sign up fifty guys. So what's bothering you?"

Charlie blew softly across hid coffee cup. "The problem is that I'm scared to death."

**The letters J-O-B stand for jilted, obsolete and broke, so take charge of your own destiny.**

Nick's laughter boomed off the walls and the ceiling. "That's good, Charlie, that's real good. Better scared than stupid! Most of the time I went into that ring," and Nick pointed to an old poster that had a picture of a boxing ring superimposed with photos of Nick and some long-forgotten opponent, "I was scared. I could never make the fear go away, so I figured I might as well make friends with it. As long as it was going to hang around, I thought I should at least put it to work. And I did. I made fear my ally."

Charlie had never seen Nick sit still for more than a few minutes, and today was no exception. Now he stood up and shadow-boxed an unseen opponent, throwing a left-right-left combination, and finishing with a sharp upper cut. "Fear is quite an opponent, Charlie. Mine's not as tough as he used to be, but he's still there. Every day. Every time my accountant walks through the front door. Every time the Pink Slipper runs a new ad campaign. Fear's still there, telling me that the fight's not over yet, so I better not let down my guard."

"How do you do that?" Charlie asked. "Make fear your ally? How do you make adversity your teacher? If they're going to show up for the fight anyway, I'd sure like to have them in my corner."

Nick folded his arms and looked towards the door. "You've got the hard part figured out already, Charlie, which is more than a lot of the macho studs out there right now have done."

Charlie shook his head. "I'm not sure I understand, Nick."

"You've seen the young bulls out there with those t-shirts that say *No Fear*?" Charlie nodded, and Nick responded with a contemptuous snort. "No fear means no courage. Someone with no fear may be reckless, but they're not brave. No fear, no courage. Big fear, big courage!"

**No fear means no courage. Someone with no fear may be reckless, but they're not brave. No fear, no courage. Big fear, big courage!**

Nick sat back down again and drank some coffee. "Early in my fighting career, I developed my own formula for making fear my ally and for making adversity a teacher. I teach that formula to all these young people who come into the gym's youth program. I tried to get the local school system to build it into the curriculum, because too many kids are scared today, and no one's teaching them how to handle it." Nick shook his head and popped back out of the chair. "They laughed at me. Said it wasn't their job. But they're wrong; it darn well should be their job."

Nick picked up a book from his desk and tossed it on the table in front of Charlie. "Have you read that yet?" Charlie shook his head. "Well, you should. It'll teach you how to worry well." Charlie picked up the book and read the cover – *Worry* by Edward R. Hallowell. "You know what he says is the biggest learning disability of all? Worse than dyslexia, worse than attention deficit disorder?" Charlie shook his head. "Fear. When you're afraid, you don't learn. Fear and curiosity are mutually exclusive. I'll tell you this, we'd have a lot fewer kids in trouble if the schools would teach emotional skills for courage and perseverance alongside the three R's. That's another reason why I have all my kids memorize *The Self-Empowerment Pledge*.

Oh, they complain at first, but in later years I've had them tell me it's the most important thing they've ever done." Nick walked over to a table on the corner and came back with a laminated card, which he handed to Charlie. "Memorize these promises, Charlie, internalize them, make them part of the fabric of who you are. Every single day, you make that day's promise to yourself and you keep making it until you start keeping it. That's the sort of empowerment that no one can take away from you, not ever."

# THE SELF-EMPOWERMENT PLEDGE

### Monday's Promise: Responsibility

I will take complete responsibility for my health, my happiness, my success, and my life, and will not blame others for my problems or predicaments.

### Tuesday's Promise: Accountability

I will not allow low self-esteem, self-limiting beliefs, or the negativity of others to prevent me from achieving my authentic goals and from becoming the person I am meant to be.

### Wednesday's Promise: Determination

I will do the things I'm afraid to do, but which I know should be done. Sometimes this will mean asking for help to do that which I cannot do by myself.

### Thursday's Promise: Contribution

I will earn the help I need in advance by helping other people now, and repay the help I receive by serving others later.

### Friday's Promise: Resilience

I will face rejection and failure with courage, awareness, and perseverance, making these experiences the platform for future acceptance and success.

### Saturday's Promise: Perspective

I will have faith that, though I might not understand why adversity happens, by my conscious choice I can find strength, compassion, and grace through my trials.

### Sunday's Promise: Faith

My faith and my gratitude for all that I have been blessed with will shine through in my attitudes and in my actions.

Nick sat back down again as Charlie read the seven promises, only this time he pulled his chair up against the table as though he intended to stay for a while. Pulling a yellow pad in front of him, he sketched a square and a diamond. "The one thing you must never lose," he said, "is your hope. On this paper I've drawn the despair square and the hope diamond. The despair square," and as he spoke he traced the four corners of the square, "is *despair* leading to *pessimism* leading to *inaction* leading to failure." Now he moved his pen to the diamond. "The hope diamond is *hope* leading to *optimism* leading to *action* leading to success. Without hope, it's hard to find courage."

**Courage and energy go hand-in-hand. Courage without energy is nothing but good intentions. Energy without courage is as likely to run away as it is to stand and fight.**

"You also need energy. Courage and energy go hand-in-hand. Courage without energy is nothing but good intentions. Energy without courage is as likely to run away as it is to stand and fight. That's why your business plan had better include renewing your membership in the Downtown Gym, Charlie! You better get in shape so you can have the energy to fight fear. Fear can be an ally if you subdue it, but if you don't, it will be the most deadly enemy you ever face."

Charlie smiled sheepishly. "I'll be in on Saturday with a check, Nick. But I'm not really sure what you mean when you say that fear can be an ally. My fear has always seemed like the worst of enemies."

"Fear can be an ally in four different ways," Nick responded. "First, it can simply be a warning that you're not ready for something. Whenever I climbed into the ring, the magnitude of my fear usually had more to do with how well I'd prepared than with the caliber of my opponent. When my legs and my belly were strong, I could stand in there with anyone; when I'd cheated myself by slacking off on training, I knew I could get knocked out by a nobody from nowheresville who happened to toss a lucky punch in my direction."

Nick rubbed his jaw as though feeling the residue of an ancient knockout blow. "When you're running a business, man, there's a lot to be afraid of. Of course, you can always run out of money. And you can run out of time. You can get cheated by your employees. If you're not a good boss, you can end up cheating your employees. So you take an accounting course and discipline yourself to look at the books at the end of every day so you won't run out of money. That makes fear of bankruptcy your ally. You read a book on time management and you stop watching TV so you have time to watch your business. That makes fear of deadlines your ally. You do a better job of screening new employees to make sure they fit the values you want your company to stand for, and you spend time getting to know them and building up their trust. That makes fear of getting cheated your ally. And you learn how to become a better leader, someone who doesn't just care about making the most money, but is even more concerned about making the most of his people. That makes fear of inadequacy your ally. And so on and so on."

Listening to Nick speak now, Charlie could hardly imagine that he once made a living by pummeling other human beings into senselessness.

"The second way fear can be an ally is that it can tell you when you're on the wrong path in life. When your heart is pulling you in one direction, but your feet are following the paycheck in another, you're going to live with a lot of fear. I'm guessing that the last year or so at LPI you suffered from a sort of chronic dread. Am I right?"

"Knockout!" Nick smiled.

"That's because your heart didn't belong there but your ego didn't want to believe it. You were to used to the paycheck and the perks. But when the emotional price you were paying for the pay and the perks started to escalate, your fear started to rise. That kind of fear is like a cancer that will eat away at you, and as long as you keep walking down the wrong path it will never be your ally. But once you turn around..."

Nick paused for a moment, then pointed at Charlie.

"You told me you were terrified when you walked out of the bank today, but you had the wrong diagnosis. What you were really feeling was the exhilaration of a new beginning, like a kid about to go on a roller coaster for the first time. That's the magic that transforms fear into an ally. Look at the card again, and read Wednesday's Promise on Determination."

Charlie did as he was told, then Nick continued. "The third way fear can be an ally is when you recognize it as a call to action. When I had my shot at the title, I got a videotape of some of Alport's biggest fights. Alport never had the notoriety of Hagler or Hearns, but I'll tell you, he was every bit as tough. When I watched tapes of him punching a man into a meatball, my blood turned to ice." Nick was silent for a moment. "You know, Alport killed a man once. They were just sparring, for heaven's sake. The other guy had on a helmet and everything. Alport hit him so hard they say he was dead before he hit the canvas. And I had to go into the ring with that man! I was scared, of course, but I was also proud. I didn't just want to live through that fight, I wanted to win it. I trained like a monster. When the opening bell sounded that night in Madison Square Garden, I was faster and stronger and more confident than I'd ever been in my whole life."

Nick momentarily retreated into his memories, his gaze on a poster taped to the far wall. "I'll never forget the way Alport tried to stare me down. There was murder in his eyes; it seemed that the ref's instruction took three hours that night. But you know, something funny had happened: my fear had become hard, just like I was. Like iron forged in the fire, my fear was transformed into an angry determination."

Nick's eyes went soft as he relived his moment under the spotlight. "It went all fifteen rounds – that was back in the days that championship fights were longer, you know." Nick had a sort of melancholy smile, nostalgia without regret. "He beat me pretty convincingly that night, Charlie, but I won the bigger fight. I won the respect of my fear. And we've had a pretty good relationship ever since."

Nick brought the coffee pot over and refilled both cups. "The fourth way fear can be an ally is most important. Fear can be a call to faith. The things we're most afraid of, like dying, are things we really can't do anything about. So we make a choice. Do we face dying with fear or do we face it with faith? Every time I went through those padded red ropes into the ring, I crossed myself and left my life in God's hands. And you know what? Even though the other guy in the ring was determined to hurt me as bad as he could, I've never felt safer in a funny sort of way, like God was telling me he wasn't done using me in this world just yet, and to go out there and do my best and leave the outcome to him. God never let me down."

Nick was back in his chair, but squirming like he wouldn't be sitting still for very long. "Today I'm afraid of different things, of course. No one is trying to knock my head off, at least not in a physical sense. In business, it's things like rejection and failure we're afraid of, not getting a physical beating. But you know what? It's like I tell my kids." Nick was back up, marching over to the wall adorned with pictures of his young charges. "Rejection is like the red badge of courage. It may hurt for a while, but the more rejection you're willing to take, the more successful you can be. Cowards don't get rejected very often, because they don't even try. And failure is like the medal of honor. You can be a hero if you try something and fail, but you'll never make anything of yourself if you avoid failure by failing to try."

Charlie looked over at the wall of fight photos. There in the center was a black and white picture of Nick and another man standing inside a boxing ring, separated by a referee. Nick's face looked like it had been run over by a Sherman Tank. The ref was raising the other man's hand, but something in Nick's expression told you that he had won the bigger fight that night. He stood proud and tall, beat-up but unbeatable.

"I've heard you talk about twelve steps of courage and perseverance, Nick. Can you tell me what they are?" Charlie had been making notes in his steno pad, and turned to a new page.

"Certainly," Nick replied. He cracked his knuckles loudly, then shook his head as if to say I gotta stop doing that one of these days. "There are six each – six steps for courage and six steps for perseverance. The first step to building your courage is understanding your fear, to identify it. If you give fear a name, it becomes just a problem, and it's a lot easier to solve problems than it is to conquer fear. Let me give you an example. Johnny Dolan is one of the kids in our after-school program. He comes in the other day and shows me his report card. It's terrible! The boy's darn near flunking out of school. And he's afraid his daddy's gonna give him a whipping. So I asked him what the problem was. He says that his daddy's gonna whup him. No, I said, that's your fear. The problem is that you're not doing very well in school. I asked him to write down a list of things he could do to fix the problem – like spending more time studying instead of watching TV, or asking his teachers for help. Then I told him to circle the ones he was willing to make the commitment to do. Well, you wanna know what happened?"

Charlie nodded.

"When Johnny showed his daddy that report card plus his plan of action for making it better the next time, not only did he not get a whippin', his daddy actually took him right down to the office supply store to buy him a new organizer, because being disorganized was part of the problem he identified. Fear is imaginary, so you can't really make it go away, but problems are real. You can fix them, and then fear becomes your ally." Nick held a fist to his chest and nodded.

"The second step is to talk to your fear, to understand what it's trying to tell you. When I decided to expand, to go from being just a gym for tough street kids to being an upscale health club, it was the scariest time of my life. I'd wake up in the middle of the night with a knot in my stomach. That never happened when I was boxing, not even before the big fights. Finally, I decided to have a conversation with my fear, ask it what the problem was."

Nick looked at Charlie as if to make sure he didn't think this was too silly, then went on. "You know what my fear told me?"

"What?"

"That my laziness was going to get me into big trouble. See, up to that point I had just assumed that running a health club would be pretty much like running a gym, but on a bigger scale. But my subconscious mind, and the fear it was creating, wasn't so sure. It wanted me to do some market research, to interview a couple dozen health club owners in other cities, and maybe to hire a consultant who specialized in that area, before I started pouring my life savings into a new building. You know what happened to my fear when I started doing all those things?"

"It went away?"

"Where have you been for the last hour!" Nick bellowed. "Have I been talking to a wall or something! Fear never goes away, at least not in this world. It became my ally. Whenever I'd feel the fear come back again, I talked to it. 'What do I have to do to convince you this time?' I'd ask it. And it would tell me. Sometimes," Nick continued, going back to pacing the room, "fear wouldn't like my answer. And then I had a choice: either to give into the fear and not do what I was about to do, or to talk back to it, to put it in its place. You'll be amazed at how cowardly fear can be when you stand up to it." Nick glared over at Alport's picture on the wall, and Charlie wondered if he kept it up there just to keep himself motivated.

"The third step is to get connected. If you're trying to do something important, you'll never do it alone. The feeling of being alone against the world can be one of the most frightening experiences anywhere. When I was a fighter, I had a whole team in my corner, and I had a coach. I still do have a coach. Only now, it's a business coach, someone who can teach me new skills and knowledge, help me stay on track, and give me a new perspective on my problems and my opportunities. I spend four or five hours every week networking, meeting new people and building better relationships with people I already know. The more connected I feel to other people, and the more people

**If you're trying to do something important, you'll never do it alone. The feeling of being alone against the world can be one of the most frightening experiences anywhere.**

I know understand and support my dreams and goals, the more courage I seem to have."

"Who's your coach," Charlie asked, "and what are some of the groups you belong to?"

"You ever hear of Ryan Bennett?"

"The bedroom billionaire?"

Nick laughed. "You read his book, huh?"

"Yeah. Pretty amazing, how a guy turned a business he started in his bedroom into a billion dollar empire."

"Yep. Well, back when he was just getting started, he had this coaching program. He'd meet with a group of us every month, share his wisdom, give us homework, critique our business plans, and mostly just give us the shot in the arm and the kick in the ass we all needed to get moving. Now, of course, he's got a whole team of people he's trained to be coaches using his philosophy. And I've stayed with the program, year after year."

"Don't you ever reach a point where you don't need it anymore?"

"Charlie, think of the greatest professional athletes who ever played in any sport: Ali, Joe Montana, Flo-Jo, Michael Jordan, Kathy Rigby. Name any one of them who got so good they didn't need a coach anymore. Just one."

Charlie was silent.

"No matter how good you think you are or how much you think you know, one of the best investments you can ever make is having a good coach in your corner.

"After you get connected to *people*, the fourth step is to become detached from *things*. The more attached you are to your possessions, your lifestyle, your job, the more you set yourself up for living with the fear that you might lose all those things. And the more attached you are to having things turn out the way you want them to turn out, the more you'll feel the dread that they'll turn out some other way. Be thankful for what you have when you have it, but don't mourn the loss if you should lose it. Have wonderful dreams and work hard to make them happen, but don't cry if the outcome is different than what you had hoped for. It's like they say at AA – Let Go and Let God. There are a lot of people in this gym today who say they would give their eye teeth to do what you're doing – start their own business. But they're not willing to pay the price, to give up the big house and the luxury car. You might say they no longer live in a house or drive a car; they live in a prison and get from one place to another in a jail on wheels. They've become prisoners of their possessions. No wonder fear is never far below the surface in their lives." Nick shot a quick left-right at an unseen foe.

"Step number five is to lighten up and have more fun. It's hard to be frightened when you're laughing. You know, I used to enjoy watching Ali more than any other boxer, but not just because he was the best – which he was. He was like… like joy in motion. Not just in the ring, but all the time. When he was training, when he was clowning around at the weigh-in, during interviews. Part of the reason the man seemed so fearless is that he was always having fun! When I decided to expand in the health club business, I used to hate making cold calls to sell memberships. And because I hated it, I wasn't any good at it. I knew I had to find a way to make it fun. Well, you know me, I'm a sarcastic S.O.B. who's still pretty rough around the edges, and I get a kick out of giving people a hard time. So I just started doing what comes naturally to me. Walking up to people and insulting them."

Charlie looked aghast and Nick just laughed.

"Really! I did. I'd walk up to some potbellied businessman waiting for a cab and say, 'Hey, fatso, why don't you get in shape so you can get a life.' Then I'd hand him a card for a free one-month membership at the gym. Or I'd walk up to a lady smoking in a bar, hand her a card, and say, 'Why don't you work on getting curves instead of working on getting cancer?'"

"You didn't!"

"Sure did! Pretty soon I was the talk of the town. I was on all the TV news shows. Even had *Sports Illustrated* wanting to do a story about me, but they backed off when I called the publisher to tell him what a rotten thing it was for a sports magazine read by almost every kid in America to be pushing smoking the way it does."

"Did anyone ever pick a fight with you?"

"Hell, no! Look at this face," Nick commanded, pointing to his lopsided nose. "Would you start a fight with some guy wearing a Golden Gloves t-shirt and this face?"

"No way!" Charlie exclaimed.

"Actually, one time I was in a bar handing out cards, and this guy, whose table I'd passed by without stopping, comes up to me and says, 'What's the matter? Aren't I fat enough for ya? Look at this gut,' he said, pointing at his belly. 'How come I don't get a card?' Well, I gave him one, and two months later he made membership a free benefit for everyone in his company. Now he's my biggest account." Nick laughed explosively and it struck Charlie that fear didn't stand a chance against that kind of humor.

"The last thing, point number six, is that you've got to have faith. Like I said earlier, the biggest fears aren't so much conquered as they are accepted. When you have faith in the meaning of life, in the individual purpose of your existence, and in the benevolent hand of the Creator, you begin to see how so many of the things you're most afraid of, the adversities of life, are really to your ultimate benefit."

Nick stood and stretched and cocked his neck left and right several times, the way Charlie had seen fighters do it on TV when they were facing each other down during the ref's instructions. "And that brings me to the second half of the formula – making adversity your teacher. The first step is simply to expect it. It's funny how, when something bad happens to someone, they take it so personally, as if somehow bad things should only happen to other people. They should read the Twenty-Third Psalm again. It says we go *through* the valley of the shadow of death – not over it, under it, or around it – through it. Jackie Meyers was one of my greatest mentors in the fight game. Here's what he taught me to say when adversity strikes: 'I knew you were coming, adversity, I was just hoping you wouldn't come quite so soon. But as long as you're here, we might as well sit down and talk. What lessons have you brought me? How are you going to make me stronger?' That attitude always helped me keep my perspective when things seemed to go wrong. The second step, though, is to realize that even though we must eventually all go *through* the valley of the shadow of death, we don't need to camp out down there in the darkness."

Charlie laughed. "You'd be amazed," Nick responded, "how many people actually take up permanent residence down there. It's more comfortable for them to be down in the valley, because then their expectations can be so low. It takes a lot less energy to be miserable than it does to be happy, so they just wallow around in the valley, moaning about how terribly the world treats them, and blaming everybody but themselves for their problems. People like that become adversity magnets. The longer they hang around down in the valley, the more bad stuff rolls down the hill on top of them."

Charlie thought of Ingrid, who'd worked several cubicles away from him at LPI. Every day, she seemed to have a new tale of woe. An adversity magnet. The title fit her like a glove. She lived to complain.

"The third step is to see adversity as an advertisement for opportunity. The rainstorm that ruins a picnic also bring flowers and rainbows. The best time to invest is when the stock market hits bottom." Nick looked over to the wall upon which hung the pictures of the young men who had graduated from his gym. "I invested in those kids," he continued, "when they had hit bottom. The dividends I've reaped are beyond counting. You know, after people get fired, they spend a lot of time down here working out at the gym. I think it's a way they can get away from their problems and do something that builds up their self-esteem by getting physically strong – no heartless boss can ever take away your health or your strength. It's pretty funny, because at first they're all really depressed, like it's the worst thing in the world. Of course, when I see them a couple of years later and ask how things are going, what do you think they say about having lost the old job?"

"It was the best thing that ever could have happened?"

"Absolutely! One hundred percent of the time. And that gets me to the fourth step. It's from the title of a book by Father Michael Crosby: *Thank God Ahead of Time*. No matter what happens to you, there's always something to be thankful for. You can avoid so much pain and misery in your life by adopting that attitude. The fifth step is to stay grounded in the present, to be thankful for what you have instead of agonizing over what you've lost. Remember the fire we had here seven or eight years ago?"

Charlie remembered it well. It was a miracle that no one was hurt.

"Well, one day, without really thinking about it, I found myself praying for recovery, as if God might come down from Heaven and personally restore what had been lost. Suddenly, a phrase popped into my head from The Lord's Prayer: *Give us this day our daily bread*. It struck me like thunder: there's no mention in that prayer of tomorrow's bread! My gym had nearly burned down, but I still had bread to be thankful for. It's a real paradox: the more thankful I am for today's bread, the more certain I can be that tomorrow will bring a rich harvest. On the other hand, the more I worry about tomorrow's harvest, the less I appreciate the bread I have today. And when I don't appreciate today, tomorrow is not as good either."

**Sometimes the only difference between winners and losers is that the losers quit rather than work their way through the chaos.**

Nick's phone rang but he ignored it. "Number six is to recognize apparent failure in the middle. I read somewhere that everything can look like a failure in the middle, and it struck me as one of those great eternal truths. When you get started on some new project, everybody's all excited and your success seems assured. After the final bell has rung, you know whether you won or lost. But in the middle things can get pretty chaotic. Sometimes the only difference between winners and losers is that the losers quit rather than work their way through the chaos. You've got to keep moving, Charlie, both physically and emotionally. You've got to do those things you don't want to do." Nick laughed. "Being a good Catholic boy, there have been many days I've been tempted to think that I could just go to the chapel and light some candles and pray, and that I'd be delivered from all my problems. As a matter of fact, that formula almost always works – as long as when I'm done praying, I go back out and do the most important thing for me to do, which is often the thing I least want to do. I always think of the 3-P's of perseverance. They are Purpose, Passion, and Patience. That's what Never Quit is all about. Know what your purpose is, be passionate about it, and be willing to be passionate for as long as it takes to make the vision become real."

Nick got up and walked over to his desk and pulled a small pad out of the top drawer. He wrote something on the top page, ripped it off, and handed it to Charlie. "Speaking of doing things you don't want to do," he said, "this is a gift certificate for our pro-shop. I want you to go over there right now and cash it in for some shoes, shorts, and a t-shirt. Then get your fat ass out there into the exercise area and go to work." Nick waved his arms as if to sweep Charlie out of the room, then he smiled. "While you're out there, talk to as many people as you can about this idea of yours for a courage place. I'd be real interested in starting one here."

Twenty minutes later, Charlie was peddling an exercise bike wearing a bright yellow Downtown Gym t-shirt. Turning to the person on the bike next to him, he smiled and asked, "So, how long have you been out of work?"

The other man shot back a surprised look. "How did you know that?"

Charlie's smile broadened. He had the feeling he might have just recruited his first customer for The Courage Place.

CHAPTER SEVEN

# THINK BIG, START SMALL

Most of the people I know who call themselves entrepreneurs aren't entrepreneurs at all – they've started businesses, but they're still employees. And often, they're employees with high risk, high hassle, low pay jobs working for a boss who's so demanding and unreasonable that almost anyone else would have quit a long time ago. That boss is themselves."

Dr. Jared Mitchell was a true entrepreneur. While still a surgery resident at the University of Michigan, he had developed a regimen of vitamins and mineral supplements that seemed to help many of his patients recover more quickly after surgery. Although it took a long time for the mainstream medical establishment to accept him and his insistent calls for doctors to pay more attention to nutrition, emotional health, and spiritual faith in the healing process, he quickly gained a following among the younger residents and medical students.

"Contrary to what most people think," he continued, "real entrepreneurs are not particularly concerned with making a lot of money. It's certainly a nice by-product of their success, and more important, it's the fuel they need to keep building their dreams, but it's not the end goal in itself. The thing that drives the true entrepreneur is creating something of lasting value, and leaving an enduring legacy – building something that keeps growing long after they've left the scene."

Even before he'd finished his residency, Dr. Mitchell's Total Health Prescription, as it came to be known, sparked a sort of revolution within the hospital. Because there were no prescription drugs involved, it did not require a doctor's order. Therefore, anyone could recommend it to a patient. Increasingly, nurses, residents, even medical students were doing just that. Mitchell began packaging his "prescription" in a simple box containing seven bottles of pills, a book, and several audiotapes. He priced it at $18.95, and in the first month sold over a thousand of them.

"The other thing entrepreneurs do is relentlessly seek leverage. With every new idea, with every relationship, they're asking themselves 'How do I multiply this?' They have a gut level understanding that they themselves are the biggest bottleneck to building something magnificent, so as quickly as possible they begin setting up systems and structures that allow them to get themselves out of the way of their own success."

By the time Mitchell had finished his residency, his company was selling over a million dollars a year of Dr. Mitchell's Total Health Prescription. This was especially remarkable because it was being done with no advertising, no sales force, and no retail presence. It was all by word-of-mouth.

"After sales took off in those first couple of months, I knew we had tapped into something huge. I even had some of the drug companies come along asking about licensing the system. It was quite an ego builder. In fact, that was my biggest challenge in those early days – keeping a reign on my ego so I didn't get carried away and grow too fast. I had a big sign printed up that I hung in my office – it's the one on the wall over there:

THINK BIG
START SMALL

Charlie had noticed the sign, now properly framed, when he came into Mitchell's office. He'd been referred by Wilma Osterberge, a Saint Johns classmate who was now one of the top distributors for Body Spirit, the name Mitchell had chosen for his company. Charlie had read everything he could about Jared Mitchell and Body Spirit. This was a meeting that could put The Courage Place on the map.

"When the drug companies tried to buy me out, the two things they promised were promotion and delivery systems. But the price I would have had to pay would have meant total loss of my independence. I could have made a lot of money, but I would have no longer been an entrepreneur. I went out and hired a big time consultant, someone who specialized in business strategy. He came back with a report that essentially said the only way I could avoid being eaten alive by the drug companies, who could have quite easily developed their own product line, was to grow as big as possible as fast as possible. That brilliant advice cost me twelve grand."

"So what did you do?" Charlie asked.

"What any good entrepreneur would do: the exact opposite of what he recommended. For the next year, I went underground. I deliberately downplayed the product, even made it difficult to find."

"Why'd you do that?"

"Two reasons. First, I wanted any potential competitor to think I'd crashed and burned, that I'd surfed a fad right into the beach. I even hired a publicist to plant stories in the pharmaceutical trade press about how I'd had to lay off half of my employees, which was a real joke, because back then I didn't have any employees. But they bought it hook, line, and sinker. The buy-out offers went away, but so did the threat of being stomped out before I could get my roots down."

Although he was sixty, Mitchell could have passed for forty-five. He was dressed in Dockers and a denim shirt with the Body Spirit logo over the breast pocket. His office looked like it had been furnished with a weekend trip to Home Depot. Nothing pretentious, partly because Mitchell was almost never there.

"My company lost over a hundred thousand dollars that year, but it was the most profitable year of my life," he continued. "I interviewed hundreds of patients who had used my system, and the doctors and nurses who had recommended it. What worked? Why did they like it? How could I make it better? I hired a student from the art school to help me design better packaging, and kept working on making the formula more effective."

"I went to Oregon and talked to Phil Knight at Nike to find out how they had lined up all of the greatest athletes and top coaches behind their shoes. Then I went out and did the same thing. I gave truckloads away to key opinion leaders in my market. I went to Denver and talked to Dave Liniger to find out how RE/MAX had defined a new standard of excellence in the real estate profession. Then I went out and did the same thing. I set incredibly high standards for anyone who wanted to be associated with my company. But the most important thing I did was study the companies that were successful in direct consumer marketing. Companies like Amway and Mary Kay were revolutionizing product promotion and distribution with the oldest form of commerce: my coming to you and saying 'Hey, Charlie, I used this product and it really works. Why don't you give it a try?' And then you try it and you like it and you go sell it to Wilma. And Wilma tries it and likes it and sells it to Rudy. And the network grows."

Mitchell shoved his hands into his pockets and shrugged. "What's revolutionary about these models of direct consumer marketing is that the good companies have figured out a way to also give me as a distributor a financial incentive for getting you signed up with the company, and for rewarding me whenever you buy the product. One day I was sitting by the lake, just quietly meditating, and the picture popped into my head, full-blown and full-grown." Mitchell smiled, as though recalling something that had happened just yesterday. "That's how I would organize my business. I didn't need professional sales reps and I didn't need a slick ad campaign. My customers would be my sales force, and my product would be its own advertisement. I recruited five of my best supporters and rented a cabin on the Upper Peninsula for a week. I taught them all about the product, how to sell it, how to recruit other distributors. We talked about the incentives and compensation systems being used by all the various companies out there, and picked the elements we liked best to design our own. Today, those five people are all multi-millionaires, but of course, I wouldn't have chosen them had they only been in it for the money. They're all just as involved today as they were in the early years."

Mitchell took a long look out the window, and Charlie got the impression that he would rather be out running the trails than working in his office. "It took another nine months before we were ready to really start building the business. We had to develop computer programs, build up a product inventory and a system to manage it, and a million other things. I was on the road pretty much non-stop, mostly recruiting hot-shots like Wilma to be our pioneering crusaders. By deliberately staying small, we were able to build the foundation on which all of our future success would be built. And we've held onto that philosophy even as we've grown. You know how some multi-level marketing companies promise untold wealth in ninety days or less – often without working?"

Charlie smiled. His fax machine spit out offers like that all day long, and his spam filter choked on them. "Well, we promise our new distributors that it absolutely will not happen to them. During their first year with the company, they are allowed to recruit only five new people." Mitchell smiled. "Hey, it worked for me, and I believe in staying with what works. Anyway, during that year, we expect them to spend a lot of time with their sponsor learning about Body Spirit – and not just our products, but our philosophy and our values. Then we expect them to spend just as much time working with the five people they have sponsored, teaching them the same things. We ask an awful lot of them in that first year, and they're hardly making any money at all. But by the end of that year, they have built a team that is ready for explosive growth. Are you familiar with John Wooden?"

"The great UCLA basketball coach?" Charlie asked.

"Yeah. Everybody remembers him for winning, what, ten or eleven national titles in twelve years. They're less likely to recall that he was at UCLA for 15 years before he won his first title. He had to build that foundation. To think big, but start small. Do you know what the first thing was he taught his players how to do at the beginning of each year? Now, keep in mind, these were the hotshots – high school All-Americans from across the country."

"No, but I'd guess it probably had to do with defense."

"Nope. He taught them how to put on their socks. That's right! He'd watch them do it, rolling them up their feet just so until they got it right. He didn't ever want to lose a big game because one of his key players got a blister that kept him from performing at his peak potential. That's thinking big and starting small." Mitchell picked up a folder from the coffee table. "I've read your proposal, Charlie, and I'm intrigued. I think you're really on to something here. The Courage Place is a terrific concept and I'd like to help you. I'm just not sure how we can do it."

Mitchell dropped the folder back onto the table, and Charlie's heart fell with it. "It's the old brush off," he heard Gollum say in the back of his mind, and reminded Spike to get to work. Mitchell pulled a business card from his shirt pocket and handed it across the table to Charlie. "Bill Keys is one of my original five. Now he's down in Austin, Texas. I hope you don't mind, but I took the liberty of faxing him a copy of your proposal, and he was just as intrigued as I am. He said that if you can't get something like that going in Austin, which is a very progressive community, then your idea is DOA – dead on arrival. Won't work anywhere. But if you can get it going in Austin, he's pretty sure that Dallas and Houston will fall in line, with San Antonio coming on next. After that, there's probably a dozen smaller cities like El Paso and Galveston where he can see it working."

They'd been talking for over two hours, and Mitchell still showed no sign of being in a hurry. Nor did he seem to be carried away with excitement. He was just there, totally present, acting out the values upon which he had built his business. Thinking big but starting small. "If you really want to make this happen, Bill Keys will pick up his sword and shield and stand there beside you. But if you're only at ninety-nine percent, don't waste his time or yours. Go back to the drawing boards and keep working until you are at one hundred and ten percent."

"How will I know?" Charlie asked.

"Good question. Terrific question! The answer depends upon how much of a price you're willing to pay. There's a paradox: starting small will require a massive effort on your part. If Bill pledges his team to your support, are you willing to do whatever it takes," and Mitchell emphasized each of the last three words, "to make The Courage Place-Austin a model for your success everywhere else? Are you willing to sign a one year lease on a studio apartment in Austin so you can go down there for weeks at a time? Are you willing to spend every breakfast, lunch, dinner, and coffee break spreading your contagious enthusiasm for the project? Are you willing to buy yourself a pair of snakeskin cowboy boots and develop a taste for country music? In other words, to do *whatever it takes,*" and he again emphasized those three words, "to lay the foundation for explosive growth in the future."

**If you are willing to do whatever it takes today, you can lay the foundation for explosive growth in the future.**

Charlie thought for a moment – what seemed like a very long moment. Mitchell sat silently, conveying no hint of impatience. "I'm not sure," Charlie said at last.

"Good," Mitchell replied. "That's the answer I was hoping to hear. That means you're *thinking*. When I say 'think big,' too many people hear the word 'big' but don't hear the word 'think.' The thinking is the first step. Why don't you give Bill a call and see if you can set up a time to go down and meet with him and some of the members of his team. I think you'll find it very helpful."

Charlie nodded, sensing the interview was near its end.

"By the way," Mitchell said, "you won't have to rent an apartment in Austin.

Bill has a gorgeous home with a guest house I'm sure he'd be more than happy to let you use any time you're down there. Which

I hope will be a lot. It's big enough that you can take your family with you if it doesn't interfere with the kids' school."

Mitchell stared at Charlie, as if looking for some particular inner quality. "Your business plan is risky, Charlie. Nobody has ever made anything quite like this work before." He paused for a moment, then smiled. "That's why I like it. It's unique and it's daring, and I believe you can pull it off. I want to help you because your success will be good for the future growth of Body Spirit. But most of all, I want to help you because you're setting out to do something important – very important. There are a lot of frightened and hurting people out there, who are so blinded by their fears they don't see the opportunities all around them. The Courage Place could be a resource center for those people, a sort of health club for the soul. I want to help you make this happen because you'll make a big difference in this world."

Mitchell looked at his watch and stretched. Charlie couldn't believe it was almost noon, and that one of America's most successful entrepreneurs had just given him three hours from a crazy schedule. Charlie pushed forward in his chair, preparing to leave.

"I've got to catch a plane for LA at two-thirty," Mitchell said, "but I'm not going anywhere on an empty stomach. Can I buy you lunch downstairs? If you've got the time, I'd like to share with you some of the basic principles that underlie the Think Big, Start Small philosophy. It's not as simple as it seems."

"If I've got the time," Charlie exclaimed. "You're the one whose got to be in six cities in the next five days! I'd be very grateful for your advice, but at least let me buy lunch."

"Whatever," Mitchell replied, and reached for the sweater draped across the back of his chair.

Mitchell led Charlie down the stairs to The Burger Bar, a little restaurant in the lobby of his building. "The usual, Jerry?" The waitress acted as though she either didn't know or didn't care that she was speaking to one of the wealthiest men in the state, and Mitchell responded in the same fashion. "Sure, April, but could you tell Wally to put real peppers on this one, not those wimpy little pickle slices he used last time?"

"Sure thing," the waitress replied, "fire alarm number three. And how about for you, honey," she said, looking at Charlie.

"Well, I guess I'll just have the same," he replied.

April rolled her eyes, then made a note on her pad. "Good grief, another lunatic. Where do you dig these guys up, Jerry?" Without waiting for a response, she walked back toward the kitchen.

"What have I gotten myself into?" Charlie asked.

"Oh, it won't be so bad," Mitchell replied. "Just a grilled ham and cheese with tomato slices and a big wad of jalepeno peppers laid on top, and a cocktail made of carrot, cucumber, and prune juice. You know the old saying: you are what you eat?" Charlie nodded. "Well I figure if that's true, I might as well eat something interesting."

As they ate, Mitchell outlined what he called the ten commandments of Think Big, Start Small. "The first commandment," he began, "is to start with yourself and your own core values. I would guess that, when you think of the person you would ideally like to become, there's a pretty big gap between that ideal of the future and where you are today."

"Oh, not too big," Charlie replied. "I'd say it's bigger than the Grand Canyon but smaller than the Pacific Ocean." Both men smiled, and Mitchell said, "Keep it that way, Charlie. The day you think you've arrived, you've lost the game."

Mitchell pulled a card out of his wallet and handed it to Charlie. "These are the *Twelve Core Action Values*. Have you ever heard of them? I use it as sort of a personal compass – am I being the person I want to be, and am I doing that things that are most important for me to do."

"Well, I've seen lots of values statements, but this is the first I've ever seen this list. May I make a copy?"

# THE TWELVE CORE ACTION VALUES

### 1. Authenticity

Know who you are and what you want; master your ego, emotions, and ambitions; and believe yourself capable and deserving of success.

### 2. Integrity

Be honest with yourself and others and honor your commitments.

### 3. Awareness

Keep your attention anchored in the present here and now, and keep it centered on the positive.

### 4. Courage

Make fear your ally and always act with confidence and determination.

### 5. Perseverance

Make adversity your teacher and never give up on your dreams.

### 6. Faith

Believe that you will be supported in ways that cannot be anticipated in advance and expect a miracle.

### 7. Purpose

Define your purpose in life and perform your work with love and enthusiasm.

### 8. Vision

Dream magnificent dreams, transform them into memories of the future, plan for their fulfillment, and keep the dream alive when the going gets tough.

## 9. Focus

Concentrate your essential resources on your key priorities and avoid distractions.

## 10. Enthusiasm

Pursue your mission with passion, bring joy into the lives of others, and have fun in what you do.

## 11. Service

Share your blessings, help others succeed, and have a compassionate heart.

## 12. Leadership

Ask for help, build a team, help each team member be a winner, and create an enduring legacy.

"Why don't you keep the card. I work my way through that list every year, one action value per month. It's an idea that I believe was originated by Ben Franklin, to take one virtue per month and apply yourself to it. This is May, so for me it's Perseverance month. That's why I'm spending so much time on the road. I'm going after the potentially big clients who have turned us down to see if one more big push won't bring us the business. The only way you'll ever get across the Grand Canyon, or the Pacific Ocean, is one step at a time. So even with your own personal development, Think Big, Start Small is the best approach. Every day you make what seems like tiny little improvements. You may not even see the changes as they occur but one day you look around and realize that everyone else is looking up to you. Then, of course, you'll know it's time to cycle through the program again to become even better, because you're carrying a lot more responsibility."

Charlie put the card with *The Twelve Core Action Values* into his shirt pocket, and realized that it had been sized perfectly for just that purpose – so someone could get into the habit of pulling it out regularly. "The second commandment is that thinking comes before getting rich. You mentioned Alan Silvermane; he's been a terrific mentor for me. He often mentioned his association with Napoleon Hill, and why he called his self-help classic *Think and Grow Rich* – not *Grow Rich and Think* – for a reason, but every day I meet people who have it reversed. They think they don't have the time to think because they're too busy trying to make a living. It's like putting up a building first, and then going back to draw the blueprints. You've got to pay attention, critically observe, see the obvious opportunities that everyone else is walking right past, ask the apparently dumb questions that everyone else is afraid to ask. Then you start thinking in ways that no one else is thinking. That's when you start walking down the road to becoming rich."

Mitchell asked the waitress to bring another bowl of jalepeno peppers, saying with a wink that they kept them young. "Third, recognize the paradox that while what will be big tomorrow might seem small today, what seems big today will be small tomorrow. The tiny mustard seed that is small today will, with care and cultivation, grow into a giant tree. That's thinking big and starting small. But at the same time, the mountain that seems so big and overwhelming today will eventually reveal itself as just a foothill on the path toward even more magnificent towers that were previously hidden in the mist." Mitchell speared several jalapeno peppers, and Charlie wondered if all the vitamins and supplements had rendered him impervious to pain.

**Today is your dress rehearsal for tomorrow.**

"The fourth commandment is to start small, but to start now. Right now! To be an entrepreneur is to make lots of mistakes, so you might as well get on with it. Try things. Pursue what works tenaciously and abandon what doesn't work quickly. You've heard it said that life is not a dress rehearsal, right? Well, in at least one critical respect, life is a dress rehearsal. Today is your dress rehearsal for tomorrow. No symphony orchestra ever sounded beautiful together without first sounding awful together – it takes hours and hours of rehearsal to transform noise into music."

"And sometimes not even that works."

"Excuse me?"

"Oh, nothing. I'm sorry, but my wife is on the board of an amateur symphony, and every performance they do sounds like a first rehearsal to me."

Mitchell laughed. "Sounds like they need a more entrepreneurial conductor!"

"And about forty new players," Charlie added.

"Now, what if you were to go to one of their concerts a year from now and discover your wife's ugly caterpillar band had been transformed into a monarch butterfly of a symphony? Would you guess that the change occurred overnight, or in tiny increments spread out over time?"

"Gradually, of course."

"Have you ever read any of the work of James Bryan Quinn? He's a professor at the business school at Dartmouth College."

"No," Charlie replied. "The professors at Saint Johns were pretty insular. They mostly had me read their own books."

"Well, about thirty years ago Quinn did some research that showed the most successful business strategies weren't developed at some think tank management retreat, but rather evolved out of lots of trial balloons and small marketplace experiments. He called it Logical Incrementalism, which is perhaps another way of saying Think Big, Start Small. At Body Spirit, we're pretty picky about who we bring on-board as a marketing executive. We probably interview a hundred people for every one we bring under our wing. Now, how big do you think our company would be today if, instead of flying around the country talking to people all day every day, I'd sat in my office drawing up plans for how to snag exactly the right people?"

Charlie just shook his head.

"A lot smaller!" Mitchell exclaimed. "A whole lot smaller. And that's a metaphor for what you have to do in your business. You have to go start prying open those oysters. Not very many of them will have pearls in them, but the sooner you start opening them, and the more of them you do open, the more pearls you will find. Number six is to dream like a king but spend like a pauper. Especially in the early days of business, you've got to be a real curmudgeon. At some point, you're going to run out of money. That must be one of the ironclad laws of entrepreneurship, like running out of money is some sort of cosmic test you have to pass to graduate from survival stage to growth stage. And when you do run out of money, you're going to think back on all the money you've blown and wish you had it back in the bank. You may not be able to avoid running out of cash, but you can put the day off, and by adopting frugal disciplines now, make sure it's not so traumatic when it does happen. You've probably heard of buyer's remorse, but have you ever heard of saver's remorse?" Both men laughed at the notion.

"Number seven is another paradox. You need to be absolutely committed to your mission, but peacefully detached from the outcome. Here's what I mean by that. From the very beginning, you have to keep that vision of where you're going – I think you earlier referred to it as your memory of the future – planted firmly in the front of your mind. It has to be a total commitment, that you will do whatever it takes to make that vision, that memory of the future, become a reality. But at the same time, you have to be flexible about how you get there. There will be many apparent setbacks, some of which will be genuine reversals and others which will turn out to be blessings in disguise. It's almost always impossible to tell one from the other when you're in the middle of it. You have to have the equanimity to accept the circumstances, and to adapt as necessary, without abandoning your central purpose."

Mitchell took out his wallet and laid a hundred dollar bill on the counter. "I have a friend whose business was forced into bankruptcy, substantially as a result of outside forces over which he had little control. Still, it was a devastating experience for him. He told me later that he had actually contemplated suicide when it happened. But if you ask him today, he'll tell you that going through bankruptcy was the best thing that ever happened to him or his business. It got him more focused on his priorities, and forced him to compensate for his own weaknesses by building a stronger management team. Of course, in order to pay the salaries of the extra people, he also had to start dreaming a bigger dream, and to raise his sights and aim for a bigger target." Mitchell laughed. "One of the most closely-guarded secrets of the universe is that bigger targets are easier to hit than little ones, in the world of business as well as in the sport of archery."

Charlie tried to not eye the C-note on the counter, and wondered if Mitchell was really going to leave such a big tip. In doing his research for this meeting, he'd read something Mitchell had written many years previously, an article arguing that abundance mentality began with a spirit of extravagant generosity, not with visualizing great wealth for yourself. "The eighth principle is that you need to be very careful about who you select to be part of your original core team, because they're going to have disproportionate influence on your future development. Today, Body Spirit has over 100,000 marketing execs around the world, but guess how many are involved in making the most important decisions: the handful of people who were with me from the very beginning. They're not necessarily any smarter or more capable than the others, they just happened to be there when we were building the foundation. It's going to be much the same with The Courage Place. You'll always have a special relationship with the people who set up your first few shops, with those first few investors who believed in you and your dream when no one else would. Choose those first few people very carefully, Charlie, then take very good care of them, because they will be crucial to your future success."

Mitchell finished his carrot concoction, and looked out the window as he continued. "I can't think of anyone who built a more powerful or enduring legacy than Jesus of Nazareth. Two thousand years after his death, more than a quarter of the world's population looks to him as their savior. For the most part, he built this church on the foundation of twelve men he carefully hand-picked for the job. Commandment number nine is to avoid negative people and petty thinkers at all cost. They will bring you down, Charlie, they will steal your dreams. When the going gets tough, and it most assuredly will, the people I call pickle-suckers – because they look like they were born with dill pickles stuck in their lips – will stand over you gloating like buzzards in the desert. Stay away from them! Go out of your way to be with people who have big dreams of their own and believe in their ability to fulfill those dreams. Those are the people most likely to believe in you and in your dreams, and to help you in making those dreams become real. Just make sure that you do whatever you can to help them in return."

Charlie made a note to somehow include a pickle jar in his Metaphorical Visualization toolbox. Mitchell continued. "Number ten is more practical, and that's to build a growth contingency into your every plan. When I was a surgery resident, for a while I served on the hospital Facility Planning Committee. We were designing a new building, and the architect had marked a certain area as 'shell space.' There was nothing in it. I asked about it, and he said it was simply designated for future growth. At the time, no one knew what that growth would be, it was just a lot cheaper to build the shell now without finishing the interior than it would have been to add on later. When you start building your business, build in some shell space of your own. Hire people who are smarter and more qualified than they need to be, so they can grow into bigger jobs you may not have anticipated. Get a computer system bigger and faster than you think you'll need. Do all this within reason, of course; don't go out of your way to build excess capacity, but when the opportunity presents itself to get it at a bargain price, make the stretch. Eat frozen pizza instead of ordering out for a while. The investment will pay off if you've disciplined yourself."

"Those are my ten commandments of Think Big, Start Small, Charlie," Mitchell said as he pushed himself back from the table, leaving the hundred dollar bill where it lay. "Just one more word of advice. Don't just start small; enjoy the small things. A big thing is

**If you're not enjoying the journey, the destination will be a disappointment.**

just a collection of small things. If you don't take the time to enjoy the small things along the way, you won't enjoy the big things when they come. If you're not enjoying the journey, the destination will be a disappointment. Speaking of destinations, I've got a plane to catch. You can buy the next time."

Charlie walked with Mitchell out to the parking lot and watched him climb into a new BMW Roadster. As he drove off, Charlie read the license plate on his sports car: TBSS.

CHAPTER EIGHT

# Be The Greatest Before You Are the Greatest

Terry Robertson was the greatest salesman Charlie knew. He'd been class president at Saint Johns the year before Charlie entered. As a student, he'd sold the administration on diverting money that was planned for a new fountain in the courtyard to instead refurbish the student lounge. In his first years out of school, Terry became one of the top salespeople for a large national computer company. When they cut back his territory because he was making too much money, he quit and bought a failing chain of furniture stores. Seven years later he sold it to a larger chain for a sum large enough to be reported in *The Wall Street Journal.* After deciding he wasn't quite ready for retirement, he'd bought an auto dealership which had slipped from first to nearly last in its market, and was in real danger of going under altogether.

"I don't know, Charlie," he was saying as they walked through his used car lot. "I'm either crazy or I'm a challenge-aholic. When someone tells me something can't be done, it's almost like waving a red flag at a bull. Something in me just has to prove them wrong."

Ten months earlier, Charlie had opened The Courage Place in his home city by renting space from Nick Amatuzzo at the Downtown

Gym. True to his word, Nick had helped him start the ball rolling by personally bulldozing many of his gym members into the program. "Let me take care of you on the outside," he'd say, "and Charlie will take care of you on the inside. You'll become unstoppable!" Charlie had also been helped by lots of free publicity, including a visit by the governor, who stated that what Charlie was doing with The Courage Place was one of the most important examples of "entrepreneurship with a conscience" happening anywhere in the state.

Things were going so well that Charlie decided to open The Courage Place-Austin six months ahead of schedule. Bill Keys had helped him find a suitable facility, and had signed up as a member himself, but then gradually drifted out of the picture as he felt the pull of his responsibilities with Body Spirit. After an initial surge of interest prompted by the same type of free publicity he had received back home, the phone had gone deathly silent. He was only half joking when he suggested to his local manager that she go around insulting people the way Nick Amatuzzo had in order to build his health club business. As a result of all this, he was in an anxious frame of mind when he took his car to Richardson Automotive for service. Since the dealership was only a mile from the public library, Charlie had planned to walk over and do some research until they had his car finished in the afternoon. On his way out the door, though, he had run into Terry Robertson.

"Charlie McKeever," Terry called from across the showroom, "just the man I've been looking for!" As he always did, Terry looked like a million dollars. His blue suit coat was perfectly tailored and sported a fresh red rose on the lapel. He strode across the showroom floor as if he owned the place, which of course he did. The two men shook hands, and Charlie was again surprised to realize that Terry was shorter than him. There was something about his bearing that always made him seem taller than he really was. "If you've got a minute, I'd like to show you something," Terry said, pulling Charlie toward his office without waiting for an answer.

"Sure, Terry," Charlie said, half in acquiescence and half in protest, "but I can only take a minute. There's a bunch of work I need to do over at the library."

“The library! What the heck are you doing in the library on a day like this? It’s a beautiful sunny day, and that means people are in the mood to buy something! Why on earth would you want to use up your prime selling hours sitting in the library?”

They stepped into Terry’s office, and Charlie could immediately see that Terry had gone whole hog into the car business. There were auto pictures on all of the walls, and industry books were scattered across every desk and table surface. “Sit down. Just for a minute, Charlie, I want to show you something.” Charlie was about to sit down when his eyes were arrested by a poster of a classic red Ferrari. It had always been the car of Charlie’s dreams.

Terry handed Charlie a photo of a brand new white sports utility vehicle which had The Courage Place logo on the sides. “Where did you get this?” Charlie demanded. “That logo is our trademark. Who’s driving this thing around, anyway?”

Terry didn’t answer, but instead smiled and leaned forward, and in his best used car salesman impression said, “Imagine how many Courage Place memberships you’d sell, Charlie, if it was you driving around town in this beauty.”

When Charlie didn’t smile Terry continued, “I really believe in what you’re doing, which is why I had the fellas down in the graphics shop make this up on the computer for me. We can work out some sort of trade where you give memberships to The Courage Place to my people, and I’ll give you a big discount on the vehicle. Behind the wheel of this thing, you’ll become the salesman of the century!”

Charlie finally smiled and shook his head. “This is very nice, Terry, but you know, I’m really not much of a salesman. I’ve got a lot of other strengths, but that’s just not one of them.”

Terry widened his eyes and let his jaw drop in a look of mock amazement. “If you’re not the salesman for The Courage Place, Charlie, who is? Who is the CSO, the chief selling officer, if you’re not?”

Charlie squirmed in his chair, and looked away from Terry, wishing he were sitting at his favorite cubicle in the library. He’d planned on today being what he called a monastery day – a day where he played like a monk, squirreled away all alone with his books and his thoughts. Instead, Terry was trying to pull him back into the push-and-shove world of business – and of selling. Terry walked around behind his desk, opened the drawer, and took out a set of keys, which he dropped into his coat pocket. Then he walked back around, looked at Charlie, looked up at the red Ferrari on the wall, and back down at Charlie. "There are two kinds of people in the world, Charlie. People who are in sales, know they're in sales, take it seriously, and get good at it. Those people tend to get what they want out of life – they're the ones who live the biggest dreams." Now Terry looked over at a poster of a small family sedan. "And then there are people who *are in sales but think they're not.* They would never think of reading a book on sales strategy or negotiation tactics, would never go to a seminar on relationship-selling, or listen to a tape on the most effective ways to close a sale. And then they wonder why they're not getting what they want out of life."

Charlie looked over at the picture of Terry's sales team behind the desk. There was no doubt that *they* were all in sales. "You are in sales, Charlie, all the time. Whether you are promoting The Courage Place, raising money for the symphony, or trying to teach a certain set of values to your children, you are in sales. If you want to be successful, you cannot delegate that ultimate responsibility. For sure, you can hire other people to help you with it, but in the end, if you are not selling, nobody else will."

**Selling is the ultimate test of self-esteem. You only have one product to sell: yourself. And you only have one customer: yourself. If you can sell you on yourself, you can sell anything.**

Charlie knew that Terry was speaking the truth, and it made him acutely uncomfortable. In the back of his mind, he could see the stack of books he had wanted to read today in a neat pile at the library – unread. Books on self-esteem and emotional self-mastery. He braced himself to pop out of the chair and take his leave. As if reading Charlie's mind, Terry stepped between him and the door. "You know what selling is, Charlie? Selling is the ultimate test of self-esteem. When you get right down to it, you only have one product to sell: yourself. And you really only have one customer to sell to. It's a tough, cynical, ornery, and negative customer: yourself. If you can sell you on yourself, you can sell dirt to a farmer. Until you make that critical first sale, selling you on yourself, business is going to be a struggle for you."

Terry stared quietly at the poster of the Ferrari until Charlie's eyes followed his gaze. "It's a beautiful car, isn't it, Charlie?"

Charlie laughed. "I'd give my eye teeth to see that in my own driveway."

"Would you, Charlie? Would you really?" Before Charlie could answer, Terry walked over to the office door, motioning for Charlie to follow. "I want you to see something," he said, in a way leaving Charlie little option but to obey. As they walked out into the sun, Terry pointed to a sparkling white sport utility vehicle mounted at an angle on a display platform, as though it were climbing a steep hill. "That's your SUV," he said. "All we have to do is put the graphics on it." Terry held his arms out in front of him, fingers extended, as though building a frame around the vehicle's image. "Can't you just see it, Charlie? Parked out in front of your office? A billboard on wheels! I had my guys set it up out here when I learned you'd be coming in today."

Charlie was amazed. "How'd you knew I'd be in today?"

"Simple. Every night before I go home, I check the service log for the following day. If I see someone I know, I make a point of dropping in to say hi. You'd be amazed at how many cars I sell that way."

"I hope I don't disappoint you if I don't buy a car today," Charlie said.

"You won't disappoint me if you don't buy a car, Charlie," Terry laughed as he headed toward the lot. "You'll disappoint me if you don't buy two of them."

Charlie didn't have time to protest, because Terry was already two rows down, making a beeline for the used car lot fifty yards away. Running after him, Charlie huffed, "Actually, Terry, I'm not in the market for any cars, much less two of them." Terry stopped cold in his tracks, wheeled around to face Charlie, stuck his right fist high in the air, and at the top of his lungs shouted, "I AM THE GREATEST!" Charlie stood stunned for a moment, not sure whether his friend was going crazy or had just attended a seminar on bizarre sales techniques.

"Who said that, Charlie? Who's the first person that comes to your mind when you hear the words, 'I am the greatest?' The first person you think of?"

"Mohammed Ali, of course."

"Did he start saying it before or after he officially became the greatest by beating Sonny Liston to win the world title?"

"Probably before."

"That's right," Terry said. "In fact, today he says that he started saying it before even he believed it was true. But who was the first person he had to convince? It's got to happen in your head and in your heart before it happens in the world outside. You'll never start being the greatest until you start thinking you're the greatest. And the first step is to sell you on you." Terry turned on his heels and resumed his march towards the used car lot.

As they walked across the lot, Terry continued his lesson on salesmanship. "When you get right down to it, success in sales requires only two things: preparation and expectation. Anticipate the needs of your customer, put together a package that meets those needs, and then present the package in a way that leaves no room for the word no."

They walked across the driveway separating the new and used car lots. On the far end of the used lot, Charlie could see that Terry had already expanded the business. A large sign announced the grand opening of the new dealership for imports and exotics. As they walked past row after row of used cars, Terry continued his lecture. "Want me to tell you why I know you're going to buy a new car today?" Terry asked.

Charlie started to protest, then decided just to flow with it. "Why's that, Terry?"

"Because when I learned that you'd be coming in, I didn't sit down and ask myself, 'How can I sell my old friend Charlie a new car?' Instead, I read up on what you've been up to for the past few years. I learned as much as I could about The Courage Place, including how fast it took off here and the struggles you've been having in Austin." When Charlie shot him a surprised look, Terry shrugged and said, "The Internet can be a salesman's best friend; simply by investing a few minutes in front of the terminal, I was able to read everything both local papers and Texas papers had said about you and your business over the past year."

Terry gave Charlie a light punch on the shoulder. "So what do you think was the first thing I did this morning?" Charlie shrugged. "I stopped by the Downtown Gym and signed up as a member of The Courage Place. While I was there, I picked up a few of your brochures and brought them back to the office. I took them down to our paint shop and asked the graphics technician to superimpose your logo on a photo of that new sport utility vehicle you're going to buy today," and with that Terry gave Charlie another playful punch in the shoulder. "The monthly payments on your new SUV are going to be one third what you're paying for the billboard on Broadmore Street, and you're going to get a whole lot more visibility from it." When Charlie raised his eyebrows again, Terry said, "Yeah, I checked that out too." He laughed and shook his head, as if such a thing should have been obvious to anyone.

"So when we go back to my office, I'll go through all the details with you: the substantial discount you're going to get by signing all my people up as members of The Courage Place; the tax advantages of owning the vehicle through your corporation; and the superior quality graphics we're going to apply. But for now, let's have a little fun." They were now walking across a narrow strip of lawn separating the used car lot from the new imports and exotics lot. Right up front, parked nose to the road, was an immaculate shiny red Ferrari. Terry walked over to the passenger door, reached his hand in his coat pocket, and tossed a set of keys to Charlie.

Charlie caught the keys, fumbled them, and watched them bounce off his shoe onto the pavement. "I can't drive this thing," he said before leaning over to pick the keys up. He was going to toss them back to Terry, but the salesman was already climbing into the passenger seat of the Ferrari. "Let's go, Charlie – start her up!" Terry pulled the door shut behind him, then leaned over to push open the driver's side door. Reluctantly, Charlie crawled in. The leather seat seemed to mold itself around him, and for a fleeting second Charlie pictured himself writing a down payment check. That image was quickly replaced by one of him trying to explain his new purchase to Pam; it was not a pretty picture.

"You've got to put the key in the ignition, Charlie. Otherwise it won't start." Charlie inserted the key, but did not turn it.

"Generally, I find two kinds of people buy a car like this," Terry continued. "First are those with low self-esteem who need the status symbol to feel better about themselves. Second are people with high self-esteem who couldn't care less what other people think, can laugh off the jokes about mid-life crisis, and who just love the thrill of driving the world's finest car." Terry looked at Charlie with an intensity suggesting that through force of will alone, he thought he could get his friend to start the car. "Which will you be, Charlie?"

"There's no way I should be driving a car this expensive, Terry. It costs more than my house does! What if we get in an accident?"

"That's what you've got insurance for. I'll tell you what: let's play a game. Let's pretend your business has been so successful that if you wanted to, you could just buy this car outright – pay cash for it. You know you're not going to buy it, because what you *really* want is that new sport utility vehicle with your logo all over it. But you decide as long as you're here, you might as well take it for a spin, since it's always been the car of your dreams."

"You're crazy," Charlie replied as he turned the key and the engine purred to life. "Seatbelts on?" he asked as he put the car in gear. Easing out onto Market Street, Charlie turned right, heading for the countryside. They cruised in silence for a while, past the city limits sign and past field after field where farmers were cultivating their new crops. Always a careful driver, Charlie had to pay attention just to stay within shouting distance of the speed limit.

"You know," Terry said at last, "this new job of mine has given me a whole new perspective on the power of high self-esteem. My salespeople who have high self-esteem make two or three times the money that salespeople with low self-esteem make, and without working any harder. If anything, they spend less time trying to sell because they're spending more time building relationships. And customers who come in with high self-esteem always seem to be more clear about what they want. They spend less time choosing their cars, and end up getting a better deal for them."

Charlie was silent, so Terry continued. "In fact, I'd go so far as to say that low self-esteem is one of the most debilitating diseases in our society today, and unfortunately it's at an epidemic level. I'm convinced that just helping people raise their self-esteem would do more good for society and the economy than all of the social welfare programs put together. Low self-esteem is like emotional cancer: too often, it's an insidious excuse for cowardice and laziness. Because they don't think very highly of themselves, people assume they will be rejected, and that they will fail. So they don't even try. If you don't try to sell something, you won't be rejected. If you don't try to start something, you won't fail. The sad irony is that, because you know you've been a coward, you end up being rejected by the most important person of all – yourself; and by avoiding failure at a small level, you end up being a failure at the highest level."

**Low self-esteem is like emotional cancer: too often, it's an insidious excuse for cowardice and laziness.**

Charlie looked down at the speedometer and realized with horror that he was going almost ninety miles per hour. The ride was so smooth he could hardly feel the speed. Quickly, he put his foot on the brake and slowed back down to the speed limit. In the other seat, Terry was looking at him and laughing. "What's so funny?" Charlie demanded.

"What you just did is such a terrific metaphor for one of the most devastating symptom of low self-esteem," Terry replied.

"You mean speeding is a sign of high self-esteem?"

"Not at all," Terry replied. "What I mean is that low self-esteem is often reflected in fear of success. What happens is that people get moving too fast in the direction of their goals; they start seeing the tremendous potential they have to be a success, and it scares them silly. So they back off the accelerator and put their foot on the brake, and fall back into their comfort zone. Have you heard our ads on the radio?"

"Sure," Charlie replied, "who could miss them. You've really come up with a catchy jingle there."

Terry pulled a CD from his suit coat pocket and plugged it into the car's player, then pushed the play button. It played the familiar music from the Richardson Automotive commercials, but when the announcer's voice came on, he was not selling cars – he was selling Terry Richardson. The ad was selling Terry, the natural-born entrepreneur; Terry the tough competitor; Terry, the customer service king; Terry, the wise and compassionate leader; Terry, the world's greatest dad; and so forth. It was very professionally done, complete with music and sound effects.

"Every person on our team has one of these CDs, Charlie, that's been done especially for them. I had our ad agency do them. They asked us each to describe the ideal 'me,' and then made up the tape as though we had already arrived at that point. I ask every salesperson to listen to their tape as they're driving to work, and then again as they're driving home. You can tell the ones who are doing it; they're a lot more confident, and they achieve better results. It's like I said. The starting point to success is selling yourself on yourself. In my business, advertising is like the fuel that keeps the car running. If I quit advertising, my sales would slow down and eventually the business would coast to a stop. Well, it's the same thing in our personal lives. Positive visualization and self-talk is the advertising that we use to sell ourselves on ourselves. You need a CD like this, Charlie, and you need to keep playing it until you believe that you really belong behind the wheel of this expensive sports car."

At the next small town, Charlie turned around and started heading back. Terry continued his lesson. "Whenever I hire a new salesperson, the first thing I do is teach them my formula for believing in yourself. The first step is understanding that faith in yourself occurs in four different dimensions."

"Four dimensions? It sounds like some sort of science fiction movie," Charlie said.

Terry smiled. "Well, it does, but I'm actually very serious. It's what I call The Pyramid of Self-Belief. The first level of believing in yourself is Self-Concept. In other words, what is your picture of the universe and your relationship to it? What is your understanding of the Creator, and does the Creator want to help you be a winner, or to punish you for breaking the rules? The most successful salespeople have a tremendous faith in a loving God who wants them to succeed, and who occasionally will pull strings behind the scenes to help create the conditions for their success. On the other hand, people who view God as a punishing avenger, as an uncaring and anonymous force, or as a complete void, are much less likely to build the foundation for long term success."

The Ferrari came up behind a slow-moving pickup truck and instead of hitting the brakes, Charlie took a quick look down the road, pulled into the other lane, and hit the gas, pressing both men back into their seats. Terry hardly seemed to notice as he continued his lecture. "The second dimension is Self-Image. What do you see when you look in the mirror? The greatest salespeople have a realistic appraisal of their own strengths and weaknesses, but when they look in the mirror, all they see are their strengths. The also-rans overestimate their weaknesses, underestimate their strengths, and when they look in the mirror see mainly their deficiencies."

Terry looked down at the speedometer and smiled. "I see that success is beginning to be less of a terrifying prospect." Charlie realized with horror that he was going over one hundred miles per hour, and yet the car was riding so smoothly he might as well have been toodling down a city street. He took his foot off the gas and began coasting back down toward the speed limit. As the owner of a struggling start-up business, he sure couldn't afford to blow his life savings on a huge speeding ticket!

"The third dimension is Self-Esteem: do you like what you see when you look in the mirror? I've seen people with what you would consider modest capabilities do very well simply because they like who they are. On the other hand, I've seen very talented people fail because they just can't seem to bring themselves to like the person who looks back at them from the bathroom mirror. Norman Vincent Peale used to ask why we so often forget the last two words of the second great commandment: to love your neighbor as *yourself*." Terry laughed. "When I told that to my wife, she said maybe that's why we treat our neighbors so badly!"

Charlie laughed, then did a quick check of the speedometer. "Finally," Terry said, "the fourth dimension is Self-Confidence. Do you think you're up to the responsibilities life has laid out for you? Can you do the job? If you want to make a change, this is always the place to start. When I have a salesperson struggling with low self-esteem or a poor self-image, I never try to address that issue directly. Instead, I spend time helping them build their confidence as a salesperson: you know, how to build rapport with customers, how to ask the right questions, how to find out what the customer can really afford and negotiate a fair price, and how to close the sale. And you know what? It's amazing what closing a few sales will do for someone's self-esteem and self-image. You want to know the best thing you can do right now today to build for yourself a rock solid foundation of self-belief?" Charlie nodded. "Sure."

"Forget about going to the library to read books that tell you what you already know. Instead, start driving around town and pay personal visits to the CEO's of every company you can find, selling them corporate memberships to The Courage Place. Whether you close any sales will be a lot less important than the courage and confidence you'll build by making each presentation a little bit better."

"That's a great idea, Terry, but you're forgetting one minor detail. My car will be in your shop for the rest of the day."

Terry laughed. "Actually, Charlie, the guys in the shop told me that your car has a lot more wrong with it than they thought. They're going to need it for the rest of the week. So this," and Terry patted the leather dashboard of the Ferrari, "will be your loaner car until next Monday."

"No way!"

"I'm afraid you'll have to make do with it, Charlie. And when you go around making your calls on CEO's, make sure you park right up front and gun the engine a few times before you get out. That will really get their attention!"

Charlie was about to argue when a little voice told him that this was a gift to be enjoyed and appreciated, not rejected, so he simply said thanks. They had just crossed back over the city limits and were driving down Market Street when Terry pointed to the Golden Arches on the right up ahead. "Let's pull in there. I'm starving!"

Charlie gunned the engine for a downshift, feeling more at home in the seat of the Ferrari. As he turned into the lot he asked, "Do you want to go through the drive through?"

"Are you kidding! To eat cheeseburgers in a quarter-million dollar car!"

"A quarter-million!" Charlie was about to reconsider accepting the offer of this expensive loaner car when Terry directed him to a row of empty spaces at the end of the lot. Charlie parked, and the two men walked in. As they were eating lunch, Terry asked Charlie to look around the dining room and, based upon people's expressions, to imagine what they were talking about.

"Let's see," Charlie said. "The young mother over there is telling her children to shape up or she'll stick them in the car. Those two workmen over there are talking about what a moron their supervisor is. Those two guys in suits, one is trying to sell a life insurance policy to the other, but it's not going very well. The guy sitting alone going through the want ads with a pencil got laid off a long time ago, and now he doesn't even have the energy to shave in the morning. Over in the corner…" Charlie swiveled back to face Terry. "Not a very happy lot, are they?"

"You've heard of Maslow's Heiarchy?" Terry asked. "How it's hard to concern yourself with truth and beauty if you're hungry and can't pay the rent?" Charlie nodded. "Well," Terry continued, "most people are content to wallow around near the bottom of the food chain." When Charlie arched his eyebrows in surprise, Terry continued, "I said content, not happy. They're content to sit in here and yell at the kids instead of taking a class on how to be a more effective parent. They're content to bitch and moan about their terrible job conditions instead of learning the skills that would earn them a better job. They're content to sit here reading the want ads day after day instead of having the courage to go start a little business that would let them take some control over their destiny. It's a paradox, Charlie. Sometimes the more discontented you are, the more likely you are to find the courage to make the changes that will bring you happiness."

"Would you gentlemen like refills on your sodas?" The attendant was an older woman with a neatly starched and pressed shirt, and a smile the size of Texas. Charlie wondered if she was working at McDonald's to keep herself busy, or because she had to in order to make ends meet. "Let's see, you have a Coke and you have a Sprite, right?" The men looked in surprise at this apparent mind reader, so she added with a smile, "I can tell by which buttons are pushed down on the plastic lid." She returned momentarily, and placed the drinks on the table. "Isn't this a gorgeous day?" she asked, looking out the window. Then, lowering her voice slightly, continued, "Do you see that beautiful red sports car out there? Wouldn't that be a hoot to drive?" Her laugh reminded Charlie of the bubbling stream where he and Mitch had spent a night in the Grand Canyon. After she left Terry said, "In one of his books Bill Bennet said that there are no menial jobs, only menial attitudes. Truer words were never spoken."

Charlie looked around the dining room again. Menial attitudes certainly seemed to prevail on that day. "Before we head back to the dealership," Terry said, "let me share with you my formula for building solid self-esteem. First, you must understand that there are three elements to having high self-esteem. Begin by accepting yourself as you are, warts and all. We've all got warts, but people with high self-esteem are able to accept them, and even laugh at them. People who beat themselves up over their shortcomings and use them as excuses for their failure to succeed, inevitably end up suffering from low self esteem. The second element, however, is a willingness to change, to fix the warts. Any time you're doing something to become a better person, your self-esteem will go up. If your business is struggling, and you don't understand accounting, every minute you spend parked in front of the boob tube diminishes your self-esteem; every minute you spend taking a class or studying a book on accounting raises your self esteem."

Charlie looked out the window at the Ferrari, sparkling in the parking lot. He decided he'd be willing to spend many hours studying accounting to see that car parked in his driveway. "And third," Terry said, "is to accept total, absolute, and uncompromising responsibility for your circumstances and your outcomes. People with low self-esteem are always making excuses and blaming other people for their problems. People with high self esteem accept that they are what they are today because of decisions they made in the past, and that they will be where they will be tomorrow because of decisions they make in the future, beginning right at the present moment."

**People with high self esteem accept that they are what they are today because of decisions they made in the past, and that they will be where they will be tomorrow because of decisions they make in the future, beginning right at the present moment.**

The McDonald's lady came back and took their trash away. They each declined a third refill, so she gave them a mint. "Let me share with you five self-esteem action steps that I assign each of our salespeople." Continuing a habit that was becoming more deeply ingrained all the time, Charlie had pulled out his steno pad and was making notes. "The first is to start each day by doing the thing that's most important for you to do, but which more often than not is the thing you least want to do. In many sales positions, for example, it might be making prospecting calls. I had a poster made up that I gave to each of my sales reps. It's a picture of a hideous toad, all covered with warts. At the bottom it says, 'Eat a live toad first thing in the morning; your day can't help but get better.' That's a pretty good prescription for success – do the tough jobs first thing in the morning and the rest of the day will be a breeze. The second step is to program yourself with positive visions and positive self-talk. That's the purpose of those commercials I make for each of our team members. It's a wisdom that's as old as The Bible – your inner thoughts shape your outer world, and the way you talk to yourself shapes who you become in the future."

"A man becomes what he thinks about all day long," Charlie interjected. "Ralph Waldo Emerson said that."

Terry nodded thoughtfully then said, "the third step is to pay very close attention to what you do and don't let into your mind. It's like the computer programmers say: garbage in, garbage out. If you spend several hours a day watching stupid sitcoms in which stupid people make a mess of their lives, you increase the odds that your life will become a mess. If you end every day by sitting in bed reading horror novels, it should come as no surprise if you begin experiencing a sense of chronic dread punctuated by panic attacks. On the other hand, if you spend your time reading books and listening to tapes that are positive and motivating, you will inevitably find yourself becoming more positive and more motivated."

Terry's cell phone rang and he checked the caller ID. "This will just take a second," he said before answering. He listened for a few seconds, then replied to whoever had called, "Whatever you think, Geri, you've got my support. You make the call." He hung up and said, "the fourth step is related, and that is to stay away from negative people and seek out positive people. Attitudes are contagious. If you hang around with negative, bitter, cynical people long enough, that's exactly what you will become yourself. Wallowing around in the mire of misery with other petty, negative thinkers is a luxury you simple can't afford, not even for a minute. Spend time with positive winners, and that's exactly what you will become. And finally, number five is to be nice to other people, to have faith in them. I once heard W. Clement Stone – you know, the insurance magnate who wrote about positive mental attitudes with Napoleon Hill – referred to as 'a reverse paranoid.' He thinks everyone in the world is out trying to help him! With an attitude like that, how can you possibly not be a success?"

"A reverse paranoid." Charlie underscored the words in his pad. It occurred to him that more often that not, he assumed the worst about other people. When a customer called, he assumed it was going to be a complaint. When he called on a prospective client, he assumed he was going to be rejected. He tended to see other people as potential adversaries rather than as potential friends. He wondered if becoming "a reverse paranoid" could help him change some of his attitudes and expectations. For the most part, his mother used to tell him, you will get out of life what you expect to get out of life. Perhaps his own expectations of other people had been the biggest stumbling block to building his business. Walking back out to the car, Charlie automatically headed for the passenger side, and had to be reminded that he was driving.

"We need to head back to the office so you can sign the forms for this loaner car," Terry said as they pulled back out onto Market Street. "You also need to pick up a brochure on that new sport utility vehicle, so you can begin telling us the exact specifications you want for the one you order."

Be a reverse paranoid, Charlie reminded himself. Perhaps Terry wasn't just trying to sell another car, but really did believe that his having a Courage Place vehicle would be good for business. Charlie simply said, "Okay."

After Charlie had signed all of the forms necessary for him to use the Ferrari as his company car for the rest of the week, Terry asked him to take his steno pad out and write down one more thing, "in all caps!"

I AM THE GREATEST!!!

Charlie eased the Ferrari back out onto Market Street and headed left, towards town and the headquarters of Milltronics, Inc. He'd been putting off calling on the CEO for some time now, and thought this might be just the day to stop by. He was beginning to feel right at home behind the wheel of the quarter-million dollar loaner car.

CHAPTER NINE

# STAY ON TARGET

When Charlie asked Bill Douglas the secret of his success, Douglas had answered with a question of his own: he asked Charlie if he remembered the scene from the movie *Star Wars* when the pilots of the Rebellion were attacking the Death Star at the end of the movie. It having been one of his favorite films, Charlie remembered the scene well. "Recall how that one pilot with a round face and the funny little beard was leading his squadron in for their bombing run, and all hell was breaking loose all around them? They were being shot at by cannons on the surface of the Death Star, and being chased by fighter pilots who were zeroing in from behind. And in his flat, totally unemotional voice, he kept saying, 'Stay on target. Stay on target.' That's the secret to success in business. Staying on target. It is one of the core principles of our business.

Bill Douglas had founded Future Perfect Now nearly twenty years ago. Now, the company was a leading provider of personal success coaching, home study programs, as well as a huge library of books and audio programs on personal and business success. Douglas had been one of the early pioneers in direct consumer marketing. In the early days, he didn't have money for advertising or a field sales force, so he put his satisfied students to work. First, he gave them commissions for recruiting new students into his programs. Then, as he became too busy to conduct all of the desired programs himself, he started training former students to be trainers and coaches. As the business continued to grow, many of his students started building their own regional organizations. Rather than prohibit this, Douglas created a tiered compensation program that actually encouraged their growth.

"The target principle has two components – focus and concentration. Focus means having a manageable number of goals before you at any one time. You've probably heard the saying that you can have anything you want in the world, you just can't have everything. The more willing you are to be focused, the more you end up being able to accomplish. Concentration, on the other hand, means applying all available resources to achieving that focused goal. It means staying on target, even when the world presents you with innumerable distractions and crises that tempt you away from your target. Ralph Waldo Emerson once wrote that concentration is the secret to success in war, politics, business – in short, in all human affairs. He was right on target!"

Charlie was taking notes, as had become his routine when speaking with the teachers that he found appeared whenever he began to ask the right questions. "One of Napoleon's greatest victories came at Austerlitz in 1805." Douglas was a keen student of military history, and frequently referred to the strategies of great commanders to illustrate some concept he was trying to explain. "He was over-extended and outnumbered. His chief lieutenants all advised him to retreat and regroup in order to fight another day. Instead, he attacked. And he didn't just attack, he attacked where it was least expected, right at the center of the enemy line. His men ripped a huge hole in that line. In the morning, they turned and rolled up the Austrians, and in the afternoon wheeled around to dispose of the Russians. Napoleon was frequently outnumbered on the battlefield, but he always made sure to have more soldiers and more guns at the point where the actual fighting took place. He was a master of the target principle: knowing exactly what you want, and then being willing to concentrate everything on that goal."

Douglas walked over to his bookshelf and pulled down a thin volume. "Back in 1936, in the darkest days of the Great Depression, Dorothea Brande wrote a book entitled *Wake Up and Live!* It was one of the first self-help books of the modern era. She said that people often choose to fail by getting involved in so many different activities they cannot excel at any one." Charlie was amazed at the way Bill Douglas could go without apparent effort from citing to quoting Dorothea Brande; he must have spent thousands of hours reading and listening to audios. For him, Future Perfect Now was not just a business; it was a passion and a mission.

"People are like the old circus barker who ran the shell game sideshow at the carnival. He'd lay out three or four walnut shells on a table. One of the shells had a pea underneath. Your challenge was to keep your eye on the one containing the pea as he zig-zagged the shells around the table. It was almost impossible. In the same way, people fill up their to-do list with piles of empty shells, things that have little to do with their real goals in life. They keep all those shells moving, and it makes it difficult if not impossible for them to keep their eye on the real priorities. At least, however, they always have an excuse for why they fail: they just had too many things to do. Have you ever heard of an economist named Wilfredo Pareto?"

Charlie shook his head. The name sounded vaguely familiar, but he couldn't say why.

**People who pile their to-do lists full of trivia never get anything done, but they always have the excuse that they were too busy.**

"How about the 80-20 rule?"

Charlie nodded. He was very familiar with that.

"That's the Pareto Principle," Douglas continued. "Pareto showed that almost uniformly, twenty percent of your efforts in any endeavor will yield eighty percent of your results. For a typical business, twenty percent of the customers bring in eighty percent of the revenue. In sales, twenty percent of the salespeople earn eighty percent of the commissions. In our own daily life, twenty percent of your efforts are responsible for eighty percent of your results. And so on. One of the secrets to success is to break out of what I call

Pareto's Prison. Just imagine, if you could take the twenty percent of your efforts that yield eighty percent of your results and expand that productivity to another ten or twenty percent of your time. You would have huge leverage! By a modest increase in your effective input, you would have a phenomenal increase in your output."

The relationship between Future Perfect Now and The Courage Place had been a natural. Now in his sixth year of operation, Charlie had just opened his twentieth location, this one in Phoenix. The Courage Place had become a magnet for the type of people interested in the personal development programs offered by Future Perfect Now, while FPN customers made the most enthusiastic members of The Courage Place. For the past year, Charlie had tried to interest Bill Douglas in a joint venture to develop an FPN-Courage Place retreat center. Whereas all of The Courage Place facilities developed up to this point had primarily served a local audience, Charlie saw the potential for an operation that would attract people from across the country and at the same time give him greater access to and credibility with the corporate community. It would also give Douglas a venue for showcasing the latest FPN programs, and for making his own headway in the corporate market, which up to now had shied away from FPN in favor of more traditional sales and management programs.

Douglas was intrigued, but each time he and Charlie spoke by phone he had expressed concern about losing focus, about "not staying on target." Cheryl von Noyes had told Charlie that Douglas was obsessed with focus. "You might say," she told him, "that his focus is focus!" He had never strayed far from his core business, nor had he ever entered into a joint venture with another organization. Now the two men were meeting face to face for the first time to discuss just that possibility.

Douglas' office reflected the man. The walls were lined with bookshelves that seemed to be filled with every self-help book ever written, all carefully catalogued by author and date. There was not a loose piece of paper to be seen, which brought to Charlie's mind a picture of his own office, where for each item on his to-do list there was a corresponding pile of paper on his desk or worktable. In lieu of a picture, behind Douglas' desk was an archery target with an arrow stuck in the bulls eye. It was lunchtime, and out on the grounds Charlie could see many of FPN's corporate staff walking or jogging along the trail that snaked its way through the 140-acre campus.

Douglas was speaking. "FPN is the world's largest publicly held private corporation." Douglas looked at Charlie and smiled at the apparent paradox. "We have thousands of shareholders around the world – 133,527 to be exact – but our stock is not traded on any market. Almost nobody who has stock ever wants to sell it. The only way to get stock is by earning options through your performance as an FPN distributor. You should see our annual meetings. Imagine a cross between the Harvard Business School and half-time at the Super Bowl. And what has made all this possible has been," and here Douglas pointed to the target behind his desk, "a relentless focus on the target."

Douglas walked over to his bookshelf and pulled out another volume, and opened it to a page marked with a post-it note. "You have to decide whether you want to be like the iceskate, with all your force bearing down on the key point, or be like the skating rink, an acre wide but only an inch deep. You've probably heard about time management systems that encourage you to develop three lists – an A, a B and a C list?" Charlie nodded. "Well, here's what Peter Drucker, the greatest management scholar of all time, has to say about it." Douglas put the book back, as if to indicate he already knew the reference by heart. "Drucker says you should only have an A list and a B list, and that you should put one hundred percent of your time on the A list, otherwise you'll never get anything done. Nothing, he says, is dumber than doing something efficiently that shouldn't be done at all!"

**You have to decide whether you want to be like the iceskate, with all your force bearing down on the key point, or be like the skating rink, an acre wide but only an inch deep.**

"In other words," Charlie said, "stay on target!"

"Exactly."

Charlie looked across the room at the target on the wall. He held his left arm out straight in front of his face, as if holding a bow, and with his right, pulled the imaginary bow string back to his ear. Holding that position he said, "I'm guessing it's about twenty-five feet across your office. The chances of my hitting a bulls eye from here are slim to none. If the target was four times bigger, however, I'd be a lot more confident." Charlie shot his fingers out straight, as though releasing the arrow, and watched its imagined arc across the room. "When you're growing your business, how do you tell the difference between an opportunity that's making the target bigger, which is a good thing, versus one that is presenting you with a brand new target, which very well might not be?"

"Great question!" Douglas walked over to the target and pulled the arrow out of the bulls eye, then balanced it on his finger in front of him. "I have four arrows in my quiver. Those four arrows are attention, energy, time, and money. They are the four essential resources that every business leader must manage. If an opportunity allows me to make more productive use of those resources, meaning that the payback greatly exceeds the required incremental output, then it's probably making the target bigger. On the other hand, if the so-called new opportunity requires a great deal of attention, energy, time, or money relative to the payback, then it's creating a new target that takes my eye off the one bulls-eye that is essential to the success of my business."

Douglas laid the arrow on his desk, and Charlie wondered if he would be in the office late that evening trying to shoot it back into the bulls-eye. "Cheryl mentioned that you're friends with Mitch Matsui, the guy who translates all those McZen poems." Charlie nodded, "Yeah. In fact, the seeds of my own business were planted when Mitch and I spent a week in the Grand Canyon several years ago."

Douglas stuck his hands in his pockets and looked out the window. "I must have flown over the Grand Canyon a thousand times, but I've never been down in it. I've heard it described as God's most magnificent natural cathedral."

"If anything," Charlie replied, "that's an understatement."

"Let me know if you guys go again. I'd love to tag along, if you don't mind."

"As a matter of fact, we're planning a trip for early October. I'll send you some information."

"Thanks. That'd be great. And I'd also love to meet Mitch. I really get a kick out of those McZen poems he writes."

"Mitch swears he doesn't write them, that there really is a poet named McZen, and that all Mitch does is translate his poems from the original Chinese calligraphy. He's even shown me a few of the originals, which are absolutely elegant."

"Well, I'd still love to meet him – and Master McZen, if that's possible." Charlie hadn't noticed before, but on the coffee table was one of Mitch's latest McZen translations: *The Sound of One Hand Working*, which included some of McZen's more irreverent thoughts on work life in America. "There's so much truth in these poems, and especially this one," Douglas said as he held the open book to Charlie, who read this poem:

*Attention.*
*May I have your attention please?*
*It's a gift so often requested.*
*So grudgingly given.*
*So rarely appreciated.*

"It's like he says," Douglas continued, "your attention is your most precious resource, which is why people say pay attention. More than anything else, attention is a limited resource, because you can only pay attention to one thing at a time. People are successful to the extent that they make a conscious choice about what they want to pay attention to. Some of the most miserable people in the world are those who choose to pay attention to bad news, and never see good news."

As Douglas was talking, Charlie had been alternately looking out the window and scanning the books on the shelves. Suddenly, he burst out laughing. "What's so funny," Douglas asked.

"Another one of McZen's little poems talks about how there are many roads to success, and it's a darn good thing, too. You've built this magnificent business empire by keeping your focus on a tiny little bulls eye. That's something I could never do."

"Of course you could," Douglas replied. "It just takes discipline, and the will to succeed."

"You know, Bill, for a long time I believed that, and it was the source of endless emotional pain. Because I was so easily distracted and unfocused, I figured I must have some sort of a character defect. And finally, I read a book about adult attention deficit disorder. I'll tell you, it was like looking in a mirror; the book described me exactly. I actually went in to see a psychiatrist for a diagnosis."

Charlie laughed again as he looked out the window. "When I went in for my results, the doctor told me he had good news and bad news. The good news, he said, was that I did not have ADD. The bad news was that I had RBADD – *really bad* attention deficit disorder."

Now both men laughed, then Charlie continued: "I read a book that said that people with ADD actually make great entrepreneurs, because we're always scanning the horizon for opportunities and pursuing them quickly when they arise. We make great hunters. Unfortunately, we don't make very good farmers, because our idea of long-term planning is 'what's for dinner,' not planting something in May and waiting for a harvest in October."

Douglas laughed and shook his head. "I guess I'd never looked at it that way. I would consider myself more of a farmer, and each of the people in my organization are the plants I'm cultivating."

"Well, one of the things this book said," Charlie continued, "was that when a farmer and a hunter team up together, they can make an unbeatable combination. Maybe that would be one way we could work well together – I could bring a lot of energy, and you could help focus it."

"Maybe so," Douglas said, nodding thoughtfully. "Maybe so. As I said, energy is the second arrow in my quiver. Most people spend their energy the way a dandelion spreads its seeds, thoughtlessly tossing it out to whatever happens to be in front of them and hoping something good will happen. They spend hours soaking up the garbage on television; they carry around anger and fear and hatred, and so many other negative emotions; they drift through the day without any real sense of purpose or goals to achieve; and then they wonder why they don't have any energy. As my teen-age daughter would say, 'Well, duh!' They don't have it because they're wasting it."

"I've got my own theory about energy," Charlie said. "I think it's a logrhythmic function."

"What do you mean by that?" Douglas asked.

"Energy expenditure has a geometric impact. One unit of energy at the end of a project is worth a lot more than the same unit of energy at the beginning of a project. Think about it. When you're getting something new started, everybody has a ton of energy because they're all excited and enthusiastic. But after weeks or months of long days and late nights, people may be tired and discouraged, and energy becomes a much more rare commodity. It's at the point where you most want to quit that another pint or so of gas in the tank could push you past the checkered flag. I always ask people to imagine running a hundred yard dash. The closer you get to the victory tape, the more your legs hurt and your lungs burn."

**It's at the point where you most want to quit that another pint or so of gas in the tank could push you past the checkered flag.**

"That's a great metaphor." Douglas said. "I'll have to remember that, because the third arrow in my quiver is time."

"The universal and unsolvable metaphysical mystery," Charlie said. "I once read that time is simply God's way of keeping everything from happening all at once."

"Yeah," Douglas laughed, "well, the other day I saw a bumper sticker that said, *Jesus is coming... look busy!* If more people would turn off the TV, get their butts out of the easy chair, and get busy, then there would be a lot less anxiety and a lot more wealth in this world. So many people never achieve their goals because they kill time, and killing time is nothing less than killing life itself. Procrastination is stealing time from tomorrow so you can avoid what you should be doing today, which leaves you permanently living in the shadow of yesterday. Time is money, they say, but only if you use it effectively. And money is the fourth essential resource."

Douglas picked up the arrow and spun it around like a cheerleader's baton. "It's funny, everybody thinks that money is so important in business, but in my book it's the least essential of the four resources. One of my early mentors in business gave me some advice I've always tried to follow, and it's served me very well. In business school, we learned that ROI – return on investment – is one of the most important indicators of long term wealth creation. Most business people pay lots of attention to the R – increasing sales to grow their revenue, forgetting the fact that you can just as effectively increase ROI by minimizing the I. We have a beautiful campus today, but for many years we operated out of a warehouse with orange crates for office furniture. We had more important things to invest our money in than beautiful buildings and fancy furniture. Even today, with all our success, we are extremely careful about how we spend our money."

"More than two thousand years ago, Lao Tzu said that the sage is ruthless." Charlie was looking at the target, imagining four arrows impaled in the bulls eye. "I think if he were in the room today, he would agree that to be successful you have to be ruthless first of all with yourself. You must ruthlessly eradicate negative attitudes and cultivate positive ones."

Douglas nodded, and picked up where Charlie had left off. "You have to ruthlessly guard your energy, and channel it into only the most productive activities."

"And," Charlie continued, "you have to be ruthlessly productive with your time. Every minute, every hour, you must be asking yourself if what you are about to do is the most important action you can take to move you in the direction of achieving your goals."

"And you have to be ruthless in how you spend your money," Douglas concluded. "There are a million temptations out there, and it's easy to come up with reasons why you need every one of them. The road to wealth is built through ruthless control of desires."

Douglas looked silently out the window for a long while. The joggers had all gone back into work. At length he said, "You mentioned Lao Tzu a few minutes ago. At about the same time he was writing his poetry, the Persian army of King Darius had landed an invasion force on the shores of Greece, at a place called Marathon. The Greek army that had gone there to meet them was badly outnumbered. Many of the Greek generals wanted to retreat back toward Athens, but Miltiades prevailed upon a council of war to attack first thing in the morning. The Greeks didn't just march across the field towards the Persians, they hit them at a dead run. Speed – and concentration – made up for a deficit of arms. The Greeks swept the Persians from the field, in what might have been one of the most important battles of all time. But for Marathon, our world might not have been shaped by the thinking of Socrates, Plato, and Aristotle."

"So let's marshal our forces and move quickly." Feeling the emotion he had once interpreted as terror but which Nick Amatuzzo taught him to recognize as exhilaration welling up inside, Charlie knew he'd found a vital partner for helping him reach his memory of the future.

"Winston Churchill once said that there is only one thing worse than fighting with allies, and that's fighting without them," Douglas replied. Shaking Charlie's hand, he said, "let's make the target bigger, and then let's stay on target!"

CHAPTER TEN

# KEEP MOVING

Chuck Hartikoff billed himself as "The Coach For Business Athletes." He was a favorite instructor at The Courage Place, and now was on a regular schedule that took him to each center at least twice a year. And today he was keynote speaker for the dedication of Courage Place Convention Center, the joint venture Charlie McKeever and Bill Douglas had agreed upon almost two years earlier.

Chuck was the personal success coach for more than 250 Courage Place members around the country, and the feedback Charlie had received was tremendous. Out of simple curiosity, Charlie had sent each of them a questionnaire asking, among other things, to estimate by how much their income had increased as a result of Chuck's coaching. The answer had astounded him; the total was over $5,000,000 in the previous year. In fact, Charlie had been so impressed with the comments that he'd personally signed up to participate with Chuck's system, and had not been disappointed. Today Chuck was in his element, up on the platform, holding court for more than 2,000 entrepreneurs and executives, eager to learn his secrets of success for business athletes.

"The first thing you have to do," he shouted, leaping up onto a sturdy table that had been placed on the platform as one of his requested props, "is overcome the Terrible Too's and the Big But's! You've all heard them, haven't you?" And then in a high pitched, whining voice, he repeated the excuses that almost everyone in the audience had, at one time or another, used to rationalize away their failure to get started on building their dreams;

*I'd love to start my own business, <u>but</u> I'm <u>too</u> deep in debt.*

*I'd make more sales calls today, <u>but</u> I'm <u>too</u> far behind on my paperwork.*

*I'd go out for a run today, <u>but</u> I'm just <u>too</u> tired after all the hassles at work.*

The audience roared as Hartikoff pantomimed each excuse, drawling them out into a long, whining complaint. Charlie smiled as he looked across the crowd, knowing full well that the people laughing loudest were most likely to be seeing their own excuses ridiculed up on the stage. Hartikoff continued:

*I'd love to think and grow rich, <u>but</u> I'm <u>too</u> busy to think.*

*I'd love to have more fun, <u>but</u> my wife is such a wet blanket!*

*I'd love to travel more, <u>but</u> my deadbeat husband won't earn enough money.*

*I'd love to live my dreams, but, but, but… I'm too, too, too…*

People were laughing so hard that many were doubled over with tears running down their cheeks. By the time he was done, Hartikoff had zinged just about everybody, and most people more than once. "Until you conquer the Terrible Too's and the Big But's, your dreams and wishes will remain just that – dreams and wishes. You must change 'I would, *but* I'm too…' to '*I will, and I'll start by…*' Whatever it is that's holding you back, the excuse that stands between you and the realization of your dreams, that is your starting point. No more excuses! No more procrastination! From now on, it's excitement and pro-activation!"

**Until you conquer the Terrible Too's and the Big But's, your dreams and wishes will remain just that – dreams and wishes.**

Chuck jumped down from the table, and ran to the opposite end of the stage, then turned and ran back to the center. He turned and held both hands out to the audience. "You've got to be like a shark! You know what happens to a shark if it stops swimming, don't you?" He waited until several people from the audience shouted out responses. "That's right! It sinks and dies! And you will too, if you don't keep moving." Hartikoff again was moving across the stage. "You've got to move physically! You've got to move emotionally! You've got to move spiritually!"

He leaped back up onto the table. "I want you all to pull out your pens or pencils and start writing. The first step to getting your brain moving is getting your hand moving. One of the most exciting developments in all of science and medicine today is the field of psychoneuroimmunology. That is PSYCHO; your thinking mind; NEURO; your physical brain; IMMUNOLOGY; your body's health. What researchers have learned is that there is an inextricable interconnection between your body, your mind, and your spirit. This body-mind-spirit nexus is as essential to your success in business as it is to your success in life. You have to exercise all three – body, mind, and spirit – every single day."

Hartikoff pulled a jump rope from out of a box under the table, and began skipping rope right up there on the stage. "Being successful in business is hard work, isn't it? " When no one responded, he repeated the question more loudly, with emphasis on the last two words, and was rewarded with a resounding "YES!" As he continued jumping he shouted, "Leadership requires stamina – real physical stamina, doesn't it?" Again, a resounding chorus of "YES!"

"You've got to be tough to be a winner, don't you?" Another round of affirmations as kept on skipping rope. "But everyone else is exercising, so if you really want to be a winner, you must do more than what everyone else is doing, right?" As the audience responded, Hartikoff kicked his jump rope into high speed, and started high-stepping through each rotation. "My competition does it fast, so I do it faster! They do it for ten minutes, so I go for eleven! They do it with two legs," and Charlie let the sentence drift away as he increased the speed of the rope further still, and hopped through it on one leg. The audience roared their approval.

Charlie tossed the rope into the box, jumped back on the table, and roared like a lion at the top of his voice. He roared a second and a third time, getting the audience up on their feet, roaring along with him. The effect was so powerful that Charlie found himself hoping the architects had designed a building that would meet all earthquake standards. Hartikoff jumped back off the table and started shouting again. He was winded from exertion, so his sentences were clipped and fragmented, but this seemed to somehow add to the power of his message. "It's the old samurai paradox. When your body is strong, it will bend to your commands. When your body is weak, you must give in to its demands. Today, we have scientific proof of the old adage that a strong body contributes to a strong mind. Physical exercise is also essential for your emotional health. Pick up any book on how to overcome anxiety, fear, and worry and you'll find a prescription for physical exercise. If you're moving fast enough, fear can't catch you."

**When your body is strong, it will bend to your commands. When your body is weak, you must give in to its demands.**

Hartikoff walked to the front of the stage – his toes actually extended out over the platform – and leaned forward as if to say that this was really important, and he wanted to impart it personally to each member of the audience. "Some twenty years ago, a British researcher completed a study on the psychology of military incompetence. He wanted to understand why commanders who seemed to have similar social and educational backgrounds could perform so differently on the battlefield. Why is it, he asked, that the same military academy can produce brilliant strategists and also bumbling idiots whose incompetence causes many unnecessary deaths?" Hartikoff paced back and forth, staying close to the edge like a tight-rope walker.

"Do you want to know what he found?" Hearing no response from the audience, he bellowed, "Incompetent military commanders were unable to manage their own anxiety!" He stared out at the audience, jaw dropped and eyes wide. "Did you hear what I just said? Anxiety makes you stupid!" Hartikoff pantomimed the village idiot to a huge round of laughter and applause, then he looked serious.

"When your mind is full of anxiety, several bad things happen at a psychological level. First, the enemy's forces always seem larger than they really are, while yours seem smaller. If you would like to get a practical understanding of how this works for yourself, when we're through this afternoon, run down to Target, and buy yourself a tent, and a flashlight…" and here Hartikoff paused for effect, "and a Stephen King novel." There was slightly nervous laughter from the audience. "Go camp out in the woods tonight with your flashlight and your book, and stay up all night reading. Then you tell me in the morning how big the squirrels were!" The nervous laughter crescendoed as audience members each thought of the giant "squirrels" holding them back from taking the actions necessary for the achievement of their goals.

"The second bad thing is you don't see options that would be available to you if you had more courage. I remember seeing a cartoon once depicting a prisoner grabbing two bars of a prison cell as he peered through." Hartikoff paused as he pantomimed a sad-faced prisoner hanging onto the bars, then said, "There were only two bars! The two right in front of him. He could've walked around on either side, but in his terror, his eyes were glued on the bars in front of him. That's what happens when you're full of anxiety. How many of you saw the article in the paper this morning about the local company that had a layoff in the wake of a merger?" Many hands went up. "It's happening all over, isn't it? And it's not likely to stop happening, is it? Welcome to the future! Companies will continue re-organizing, and jobs will continue to be eliminated."

"So let's say we talked to two people after the lay-off today. The first person is scared to death – has visions of bankruptcy and homelessness dancing through his head, and wakes up every morning seeing the prison bars of fear all around his bed. The second person, on the other hand, reads the same newspaper we all read this morning, but instead of focusing on the article about the layoff, his attention is grabbed by the article saying that more jobs have been created by entrepreneurial businesses this year than in any previous year. He's especially taken by the comment that almost nobody gets rich working for someone else, and that in the previous year more entrepreneurs became millionaires than any other year in our nation's history." Hartikoff crossed his arms and tapped his right foot, which elicited the desired response from the crowd.

"Now, imagine it's two years from now. Where are those two men likely to be?" Hartikoff paused for a moment, then continued. "I'll tell you where they are; person number one did not become bankrupt and homeless. As you might expect, he eventually found another job doing very much the same thing he was doing before. And he wakes up every day with the fear it could happen again, perhaps as soon as this very day. Every time he's called into the boss's office, he trembles at the prospect of another pink slip. And of course, it's just a matter of time before his fear becomes a self-fulfilling prophecy, isn't it?

"Now the second man had the same reasons to be afraid as the first guy, but had the courage to stand up to his fears with determination. He resolved to himself that it would never happen again, that never again would he place control of his destiny in someone else's hands. He decided to start his own business. In the short run, he may or may not make more money than person number one, but at least he has set the stage for creating the kind of wealth that person number one can only imagine. Unlike person number one, person number two will never again be imprisoned in a jail that has only two bars."

"Finally," Hartikoff continued, "physical exercise is a spur to mental creativity. In a recent study, researchers gave a problem to two different groups of people and asked them to solve it. Those in the first group were placed in comfortable easy chairs to work on their problem; people from the second group were asked to ride an exercise bike while they cogitated. Guess who came up with better solutions? With more creative and more workable solutions? That's right! The people in the second group, on their exercise bikes. Think about it; how many times have you gone out for a walk or a run or a bike ride, and experienced one of those brilliant flashes where you've come up with a creative solution to some problem that up until now has had you baffled."

"Now, in addition to your physical health, you also have to take care of your emotional health." Charlie noticed with satisfaction that most of the people in the audience were writing down the new heading on their tablets. "And the first step is to lighten up and have more fun. Far too many of us are too 'dead serious,' but I'll tell you this; if you're *dead serious* for long enough, you'll end up *seriously dead*. And it happens in here first," and at this point, Hartikoff pointed to his chest with both fingers. "You die emotionally before you die physically. We all know people who are deader than cut grass, they just haven't stopped breathing so we can bury them without breaking the law."

There was laughter from the audience, but Charlie also saw many nodding heads. It seemed that almost everybody knew someone else who was "seriously dead" but had not yet stopped breathing. Realizing how much his face hurt from laughing over the past hour, it occurred to Charlie that perhaps he himself had become much too serious, and could stand to lighten up a bit.

**If you're dead serious long enough, you'll end up seriously dead. You'll die emotionally before you die physically.**

"The second thing you can do to promote your emotional health," Hartikoff went on, "is to practice living in the present here and now. Right now, there are people in this audience who are having an out-of-body experience!" There was confused laughter from the audience. "That's right! Your body is here in this beautiful new conference center with me, but your mind is who knows where, doing who knows what, and that's what I call an out-of-body experience! Ladies and gentlemen, virtually all emotional pain is caused by time travel; it's either regret, guilt, and anger from the past or anxiety, fear and worry about the future. Almost by definition, if you can keep your attention focused on what's right in front of you at each moment, you'll find the world such a beautiful place that there is no room for emotional pain. You'll also find yourself a lot more productive."

"Have you ever noticed, no matter what it is you're doing, in the back of your mind you're always thinking that there's something else more important that you should be doing? It's like the guy that's working at the office, and feeling guilty that he's not at home with the family. So what does he do? He packs all of his paperwork into a briefcase and hauls it home, to be with the family. Then all evening he feels guilty that he's not working on what's on the briefcase. Psychologists call that a double-bind – a self-imposed lose-lose." There were laughs of recognition, including from Charlie, who had caught himself thinking that he should be with his accountants working on the upcoming direct public offering rather than listening to Hartikoff.

"The third step to emotional health," Hartikoff continued, "is learning to see the world as it really is. And for most of us, that requires learning how to forget. The world is changing so fast that what you knew yesterday may not be true anymore today. It's like the old saying goes; it's not what you don't know that will hurt you, it's what you think you know that's not so. This applies most absolutely to what you think you know about yourself. The single most powerful obstacle to your future success will be the inaccurate picture you have of yourself today. Forget what you think you can't do! Forget what you think you don't know! Forget what people have told you about your limitations! Forget all the Terrible Too's and the Big But's that are holding you back!"

"The fourth thing I'm going to tell you about emotional health may sound like it contradicts the whole theme of this program, but it really doesn't. Before I tell you what it is, let me ask you to imagine that in one hand you have a hammer," Hartikoff held his right hand up over his head as though about to swing a hammer, "and in the other, you have a nail." Hartikoff brought his imaginary hammer down hard upon his imaginary nail. "Now, rather than pounding your nail in the traditional way, I want you to imagine trying to just push that nail into the wood in by brute force, without bringing the hammer back over your head." Hartikoff pantomimed trying to push a nail into a piece of wood with a hammer; he grunted and groaned and his face grew red from strain, but his imaginary nail did not move. "It can't be done, can it?" He huffed and puffed. "Your hammer needs to recoil before it can drive in the nail." Hartikoff slammed his invisible hammer down upon his invisible nail.

"The same is true for you. You have to practice what I call strategic laziness. Your emotional health demands that you have times of rest, relaxation, and recuperation. Think of a lion; the king of beasts! What does a lion spend most of the day doing? Of course! Lyin' around in the sun. Now, I'm not recommending that you try to get ahead by spending your time lying around in the sun, because it won't work. But you do need to alternate times of stress with times of rest. And here are two suggestions for doing that. First, re-introduce into your life the ancient concept of a Sabbath – a day of rest. By that, I do not mean sitting like a boiled vegetable in front of the boob tube," – laughs of embarrassed recognition from the audience – "but rather, giving yourself one day every week for reading, thinking, writing in your journal, dreaming – for bringing the hammer back over your head."

"The final thing I want to talk about today is spiritual health. You've got to keep moving spiritually, growing in faith and letting your faith shine through in your actions. I'll give you two practical and specific suggestions. The first is to pray continuously, the way Tevye does in the movie *Fiddler on the Roof.* Pray for guidance, strength, courage, compassion, wisdom, and all the other virtues you must have to become the person you want to be – the person you are destined to be. If you develop those characteristics, your success – success with a capital 'S', not just having money – in the world is all but guaranteed."

Hartikoff was about to break the audience into small groups to work on their individual action plans. Charlie looked at his watch and smiled. He still had plenty of time to speak with the accountants. Hartikoff was right, he thought. You can get a lot more done if you limit yourself to doing one thing at a time, keeping your attention in the present here and now. He took one last look at Hartikoff, who was now signing books for a very long line of people, then headed out into the parking lot where his red Ferrari was proudly parked in the front rows that were reserved for the people who arrived earliest in the morning.

CHAPTER ELEVEN

# SERVE YOUR WAY TO GREATNESS

Once a month, Charlie met with the entire management team of The Courage Place through the magic of video-conferencing. He could almost maintain the same feel of personal closeness that had developed in the early days, even though now there were more than 300 locations across the United States and Canada, with the first European center scheduled to open the following year. Several years earlier, the company had gone public by selling shares of stock to its members in a direct public offering. Now, the monthly management meeting was also open to member-owners by means of a special Internet hook-up.

For the most part, going public had been a tremendous step forward for the company. The sale of stock had provided capital that was essential for maintaining an aggressive schedule of opening new centers, as well as developing new product and service lines. More important in Charlie's eyes, when members "graduated" to become part-owners of The Courage Place, their commitment and enthusiasm increased geometrically. The downside of going public was a natural tendency for many Courage Place managers to focus more on quarterly earnings and the stock price than on the core service business. Today, Charlie wanted to discuss not just the business of service, but also the philosophy of serving.

As he always did, Charlie began by addressing some of the concerns that had been raised by managers during the previous month, and by answering questions that had been sent to him by owner-members via e-mail. Charlie used this period to get people to relax, lighten up, and think about things from a new perspective. From his years of public speaking, he had learned that before you can teach somebody something, much less influence them to change ingrained attitudes and habits, you must touch them emotionally. This warm-up period was his opportunity to synchronize people emotionally.

"Because we are in the business of helping people create better lives for themselves, The Courage Place has always attracted people who have an incredible service orientation. Now, that's a good thing – those are exactly the kind of people we want to attract. But in the early days, when we were just getting this business started, I had to continuously remind people that even though we had a powerful service mission, we still were a business, and as a business, we had to make a profit. I used to serve on the board of a local hospital, and Sister Julia always reminded us board members of her favorite maxim: 'No Margin, No Mission.' That aphorism is every bit as applicable in our business as it is in healthcare. We must make a healthy profit so we have funds to reinvest in new and improved programs to serve our clients more effectively, and to keep reaching out to bring new members into the fold."

Charlie looked at his notes. Even after all these years, he still believed in the maxim of Mary Kay Ash that the shortest pencil was better than the longest memory. "But Sister Julia's formula also works in reverse; No Mission, No Margin. If we lose sight of the mission that brought us all into this business in the first place, if we begin to let the quality of our service slip, we open the door for someone else to come in and take our business away from us. Without the mission, our margin – our profits – will evaporate." At first, Charlie had found it difficult to speak to a camera with the same passion and enthusiasm that a live audience brought forth. Now, however, he was able to quickly get into the flow by imaging the faces on the other side of the camera – the hundreds of managers participating in the live interactive video conference, and the thousands of member-owners watching on the TCP website. "My friend Mitch Matsui introduced me to the poetry of McZen. They're quirky and full of paradox, but they contain great wisdom about life. Here's one of my favorites:"

*Someone with a job is never secure.*
*Someone with a calling is never unemployed.*

"That's so true. In today's turbulent world, nobody can go to work for a company and be confident that just by being loyal, reliable, and competent they'll still be there in twenty or thirty years. Quite to the contrary, the chances of that happening are slim indeed. Even the CEO is accountable to a board, and boards everywhere – including the board at The Courage Place – are becoming more demanding, and willing to replace a CEO who doesn't perform." Charlie smiled at the fact that, even though he'd started the company, he still had to answer to someone else for his performance.

"While job security may be an illusion, finding the security of a calling is rock solid. If you see your work as a calling, and not simply the means to a paycheck, there will never be a day in your life that you can't find meaningful work to do." Charlie laughed as he continued: "Of course, there might be days when the pay is low – we've all done more than our share of work-for-free when we were between jobs – but there is always work to be done. In one of the great books of the Old Testament, Ecclesiastes goes through all the pleasures of life; material wealth, party times, power, knowledge, everything. In the end, he finds, it's all meaningless, all vanity. There's nothing new under the sun, he says, it's all dust in the wind. So where does Ecclesiastes find meaning? Why, in his work. Whatever work your hand finds to do, he says, do it with all your might."

"Much more recently, another poet – Kahlil Gibran, author of *The Prophet* – wrote that work should be love made visible. We must all strive to see our work as a calling, and to put love into that work so that it becomes an outer manifestation of our inner love for the work and for the people we serve. If we do that, I'm convinced the bottom line will grow naturally and we will all prosper. With the new responsibilities we have to our member-owners, we naturally feel more pressure to maintain profits and keep the stock price going up. Trust me," Charlie laughed, "I feel this more than anyone. I have one board member who goes on line the minute the stock market opens each morning, and then phones me up to tell me what our stock price is as that moment."

"We must manage our business effectively, but must never fall victim to the siren song of the market. There are many companies that march to the drum of their own long term vision rather than dance to the piper of Wall Street. Companies like ServiceMaster, Hewlett Packard, Johnson & Johnson, and many others have made the commitment to put their people first – to serve their employees, customers, and communities – and trust that profits and higher stock prices would follow. On the other hand, an obsession with profits, with numbers instead of people, can actually be counterproductive." Charlie went on to tell the story of Mad Dog Dunleavey, whose single-minded focus on doing what he thought Wall Street wanted cost him his job, and very nearly destroyed the company.

**Laying the foundation for real personal happiness may mean missing out on a lot of short-term opportunities to have fun.**

"It's the great paradox of service. About twenty-five hundred years ago, Confucius said that if you want to be successful, the best way is to help other people be successful. It was true then, and it's true today. Another Chinese philosopher, Chuang Tzu, said the only way to find happiness is to not do anything calculated to achieve your own happiness. In other words, to lose yourself in the joy of work for its own sake, and to helping others be happy." Charlie laughed and shook his head. "It's a paradox that I've had a hard time getting my kids to understand. Achieving real personal happiness may mean missing out on a lot of opportunities to have fun. Conversely, people who spend all their time trying to have fun often end up miserably unhappy."

Charlie took a call from one of the newer managers. "We've been asked by one of the local schools, which happens to be in a lower income community, to put together a program that will help them teach their students some of the emotional skills required to succeed in the workplace, and as entrepreneurs. I really want to do it, but I'm having a hard time justifying the resources that would be required, especially since for some strange reason, my employees are pretty insistent about being paid on a consistent basis. How do you suggest I evaluate a situation like this?"

"That's a great question," Charlie replied, "and a very important one. First of all, let me say that there is not a one-size-fits-all answer, and that you have to evaluate your own individual circumstances. Having said that, let me point out that opportunities for gain frequently come disguised as calls to service. What you need is some creative thinking. Is there a local corporation that would be willing to sponsor the program? Can you donate the program to the school, but in return have them sponsor a companion program for parents with a modest registration fee to help you offset your costs? In return for you doing the program, will the school offer membership in The Courage Place as an optional benefit to its faculty and staff? With a bit of imagination, you can often find a win-win solution that allows you to be simultaneously profitable."

**Opportunities for gain frequently come disguised as calls to service.**

The next caller was Jan Marcheson, who operated a very successful Courage Place center in San Francisco. She often asked the tough questions that were on everyone's mind. "You know, Charlie, I buy in to everything you're saying a thousand percent. But sometimes I feel like the guy who forgot he'd gone down to drain the swamps because he's so busy fighting off the alligators. Some days, I feel like a hypocrite because I'm out there in the classroom telling people to face their fears with courage and determination, and then I go back to my office and close the door and just darn near collapse under the weight of my own fears. How do you walk the talk when you don't even feel like you can get out of the wheelchair?"

Charlie thought for a long moment. "Let me say two things about that, Jan. First, you are walking the talk. There's not a person involved with The Courage Place who hasn't at one time or another felt overwhelmed by their fears and problems. If I'm wrong, please feel free to interrupt. Charlie paused for a moment, but there were no arguments. "It takes incredible strength and courage to close the door to your office behind you, to lock your fears and your problems inside, and to go stand tall and proud in front of an audience and give them the inspiration to pursue their dreams. How could you possibly empathize with their problems if you didn't occasionally walk in their shoes, or sit in their wheelchairs?"

"The second thing we must recognize is that many of us came to The Courage Place because courage is what we ourselves most needed. By teaching it, we gain it. Many years ago, Dr. Jared Mitchell shared with me a learning philosophy he'd picked up in his surgical residency, which still keeps me motivated to teach before I may feel ready: *See one, do one, teach one*. We must never forget to apply in our own lives what we teach others as part of our core curriculum; that caring is the antidote to anxiety, and service is the treatment for adversity."

"Most of the world's great wisdom is in the form of paradox, and service brings us face-to-face with some of the great paradoxes of life. Like this one: service begins with self. If you don't have faith in yourself, if you don't treat yourself with respect and have a solid sense of self-worth, it's unlikely that you're going to provide meaningful service to other people. At the same time, service transcends self. Many of you are members of Rotary, and as such have adopted the motto Service Above Self. When you adopt an attitude of service and sharing, the focus of your attention shifts from your own mostly imaginary problems and onto someone else's mostly real problems."

"A related paradox is this: you have to get out of yourself to find yourself. To achieve success and happiness, you must simultaneously reduce your self-consciousness and increase your self-awareness. In other words, to stop seeing yourself as the center of the universe, and at the same time do a better job of paying attention to how your attitudes and actions affect other people. You've all heard my lecture on the fear of success, which is far more toxic than the fear of failure. One of the most powerful weapons I know of to overcome fear of success is a commitment to serve other people. The more fervently you adopt this, the more successful you become, and the more service you can provide to other people. This will remove any doubts of whether you deserve success, or whether your success comes at the expense of others."

"I'd like to close with two final points. First, service always springs from an attitude of gratitude - thankfulness for what we've been blessed with in the past, for what we have right now, and for the future blessings we anticipate. There's nothing you can't be thankful for, even your weaknesses and the adversities that cross your path, as these often help guide you toward the destiny that is authentically yours. Finally, when it comes to service striving is more important than achieving. Someone once asked Mother Teresa why she wasted her time helping the poor, since there were so many of them, and she could never be successful at eliminating their problems. In response, she snapped that she was not there to be successful; she was there to be faithful. Ultimately, our service is a reflection of our faith. And as The *Bible* says, genuine faith is always reflected in action. It's a big part of what The Courage Place is all about."

As he usually did, Charlie ended the meeting by outlining some of the company's key plans and priorities for the coming months. Driving from the studio back to his office, something Alan Silvermane had said many years ago popped back into his head: "Dream Beyond the Dream." Charlie knew that the time would soon come when he'd turn over the reigns of The Courage Place to someone else, and he would need to start thinking about what service he would provide during the next phase of his own life.

CHAPTER TWELVE

# EXPECT A MIRACLE

Charlie sat looking at the walls of his office, which were now almost completely bare since his personal photos and paintings had been removed. This would be the last time he would sit behind his desk as chief executive officer of The Courage Place. The night before, there had been a wonderful retirement party; in several hours, Brian Hunter would move into the job for which he had been preparing himself for the past several years. Charlie had long thought about what final words of wisdom he would pass on to his successor. On the desk were four things that had been very special to him, which he would now give to Brian. The first was a simple needlepoint that Pam had made shortly after they decided to leave the corporate world and start The Courage Place. It said only:

## MARK 9:23

It was Charlie's favorite passage from *The Bible.* "All things are possible for one who believes." He had told the story a thousand times. How upon coming down from the mountain with Peter, James, and John, Jesus was walking through a crowd when a man broke through and implored Him to heal his son by driving out the demon that had possessed the boy. The disciples had tried, the man said, but failed. "Can *you* help?" the man pleaded. But Jesus turned the question right back around: "Can you help? All things are possible for one who believes." And how even two millennia after the fact, one could still feel the anguish – and the hope – in the man's voice as he replied, "I believe. Help me overcome my unbelief." And how the boy was then healed.

In all of his miracles, Charlie would say, Jesus never took personal credit. More often than not, he attributed the miracle to the one being healed: "Your faith has made you well, your faith has made you whole." And just as often, he said that any of us could do what he did if we only had sufficient faith – faith even as small as a mustard seed. Partial faith, Charlie pointed out, had been faith enough for the man's son to be healed. "I believe. Help me overcome my unbelief." Partial faith was faith enough to begin, and once you begin, faith will grow. It's not about a litmus test of what you believe, it's about having the strength to believe.

As Charlie waited for Brian to join him, he thought about how many times in the past thirty years he had been just like that desperate father, wanting so much to believe in his dreams, his memories of the future, yet struggling so terribly to silence the nagging negativity of his inner Gollum. How many times the only thing standing between him and failure had been his faith, and how often that faith was so tenuous it would have made even a mustard seed seem huge. And yet, even that tiny seed of faith had, in the long run, been faith enough.

Those first dreams that he and Pam had shared together seemed so big, so impossible, at the time. "Not in ten lifetimes," Gollum had laughed, "could you fulfill even one tenth of that vision. Memories of the future? Hah! More like delusions of grandeur." Fortunately Charlie had eventually learned how to tame Gollum. In retrospect, those dreams that once seemed so immense were actually pretty puny when compared to how The Courage Place had grown over the past ten years.

The second thing Charlie planned to give Brian was a small laminated card he had carried in his wallet from the very beginning. It was now quite worn and tattered from having been read more than ten thousand times – every morning and every evening for three decades. It was a quote by Napoleon Hill:

*Every successful person finds that great success lies just beyond the point where they're convinced their idea is not going to work.*

Charlie had made many mistakes and experienced many apparent failures. In the years to come, Brian Hunter would do likewise. Charlie hoped this small inspiration would be as helpful to Brian as it had been to him. The third item Charlie was going to leave was the paperweight which had sat on top of his desk from the very beginning. It was a piece of granite into which were carved the most powerful three words in the world:

# Expect A Miracle

Over the years, Charlie had come not just to hope for miracles and to pray for them, but to expect them. Whenever The Courage Place business plan was updated, in his own copy Charlie would print right on the cover the three letters EAM to remind him to expect a miracle. That attitude was as much a part of his business strategy as doing market research.

Charlie walked over to the window and looked out across the campus. Everything he saw had once been an impossible dream. "It'll take a miracle," one of his board members had commented when he shared the vision of a headquarters campus that would have a conference center, retreat center, complete gymnasium facilities, and the world's most comprehensive motivational resource center. Charlie smiled as he watched a crowd making its way from the parking lot to the convention center. Louisa Sheldon Henderson was speaking today.

When Louisa had come to Charlie's very first Courage Place event thirty years ago, she was a young single mother struggling with depression, bulemia, and even serious thoughts of suicide. Fewer than ten people had showed up for that program, and Charlie had felt more like crying than speaking. How could he have known that he was planting the seeds for miracles in other people's lives that far-off winter morning at the Downtown Gym? Today, one of those miracles was coming full circle as Louisa, who had since become one of the country's most popular speakers, brought her message of hope and courage to The Courage Place Convention Center. She was now planting the seeds for future miracles for others.

People so often misunderstood what a miracle is – and what it is not, Charlie thought. A miracle is not a magic trick. It's less a matter of turning water into wine, and more a matter of turning a wino into a water drinker. A miracle is usually not an event, but rather a process. A miracle is not instant relief from the problems of life. More often than not, the chief ingredient in making miracles is the simple passage of time. Jesus had said that when you pray, if you pray as though your prayer had already been answered, it will be. So often people are tempted to lose faith when their prayers aren't answered right now. What Jesus really meant, Charlie believed, is that if your prayers are reinforced with genuine belief, when you pray you will set aside doubt and worry and instead keep working and keep believing with a certainty that the prayer will be answered – probably in a more magnificent way than you could ever have imagined – but it will be answered in God's time, not necessarily in yours.

**A miracle is usually not an event, but rather a process.**

Nor is a miracle a guarantee of success or security. Charlie had always remembered reading a sentence in one of Max Lucado's books which said, "God honors radical risk-taking faith." It did not say that God will necessarily reward that faith, but in Charlie's book, it was more important that the effort be honored than the outcome be rewarded.

Charlie often heard people complain about lack of security, and he would remind them that the Lord's Prayer said nothing at all about tomorrow's bread; it asks only that we be given our bread today. Sometimes the greatest miracle was to be grateful for today's bread

– the blessings of the present – and to have faith that tomorrow's bread would arrive on time. Many of us, Charlie reflected, don't believe in miracles because they frighten us. If miracles are possible, even foreseeable, that could mean we should hold ourselves to a higher standard of expectation, but we fear that commitment.

Charlie smiled as he thought of Saint Peter walking on the water. At first it was wonderful, this being able to walk upon the surface of a lake, just as Jesus had told him he could if he believed he could. But once out there on the water, his nerve deserted him and he began to sink. What a perfect metaphor for the fear of success, the fear of commitment, that prevents so many people from achieving their full potential. We climb out of the boat of familiarity and security and start to walk out there on the water of exploration and adventure. Then, when we find ourselves achieving the miracle that for so long had merely been an impossible dream, we start to sink. The weight of fear and doubt pushes us down and we holler, "Save me!" as we frantically make our way back to the boat.

Charlie laughed softly as he watched the last stragglers running for the convention center. One of the most profound paradoxes he'd discovered during his three decades of building The Courage Place was that there is more security walking out there on the water than there is huddling inside the boat. Getting out of the boat and walking on the water, he was convinced, is what Jesus had in mind when he told us to not cover our candles with a basket. In his speeches over the years, Charlie had often said that the truth was more important than the facts, and that faith was more powerful than fear. Keep your memories of the future firm in your mind, he would say, and keep walking out there on the rough waters, because that's where the real miracles happen. Keep your courage high and your determination strong, and then Expect a Miracle.

Expect a miracle, but don't give God a deadline. Most of the miracle-making process is invisible. It's going on below the surface. When the wino becomes a water drinker, it may look like a miraculous event has just occurred, but more often than not, it's just the last stage of a long and probably painful process. The ultimate miracle is not something that happens "out there" but rather is a profound transformation that happened inside, in the head and in the heart.

Charlie's favorite movie had always been Fiddler on the Roof and he especially loved the scene where Motel the tailor, against all odds, won the hand of his beloved Zeitel. In his joy, Motel ran through the woods, singing about miracles, and especially the miracle that had happened inside of him when he stood up like a man to fight for his "impossible dream:"

*But of all God's miracles great and small*
*The most miraculous one of all*
*Is that out of a worthless lump of clay*
*God has made a man today.*

That was, Charlie believed, the ultimate miracle available to us all: to turn the lump of clay we each begin with in life into the miracle makers we are each born to be.

The fourth thing Charlie was going to leave Brian with was an eagle's feather encased in Lucite. One day, Charlie had been sitting up on a bluff looking down over the Green River. It was perhaps at the darkest moment of his life. After several years of struggling, there was the very real possibility that The Courage Place would go under. He had not even come close to meeting his financial projections, was deep in debt, and dodging phone calls from creditors. He contemplated the possibility of bankruptcy, but knew in his heart that not even that drastic step would give him the fresh start he seemed to need at that moment. In a moment of intense self pity, he even found himself wishing God would take his life, because he didn't have the courage to do it himself.

After an hour or so of watching the river flow by, his cares receded somewhat and he began to enjoy the warm sun and the soft breeze. Then he experienced a feeling he'd never had before; it was at once the tranquility of inner peace and the exhilaration of great anticipation. At that moment, there was an eagle coursing along the river in his direction. When it reached the bend, the great bird continued straight, right in Charlie's direction. As it flew over, the bird tilted slightly and seemed to look down upon Charlie. It circled back around, lower this time. On the next pass, the bird actually landed right there on the bluff, not ten feet away from Charlie.

Charlie sat still as stone, not wanting to disturb the magic. He loved eagles and all other birds of prey, and had let himself believe that whenever he saw one, it was simply God sending a message of reassurance. The bird just stood there, pacing up and down like a soldier marching in place, and then stretched his wings and squawked loudly, as if warning the world that this was his territory and he would protect it with his life. Charlie had the feeling that he, too, would fall under the great bird's protection. Then the eagle folded his wings and settled in with his chest puffed out and his head held high, like some ancient warrior rooted to his post. The breeze flowed through his feathers, and it almost seemed as if he was smiling, proud and magnificent.

Charlie looked more closely at the bird, and could see that, like every true warrior, his authority had been hard-won. His body showed the markings of many battles. Seen up close, his feathers were tattered, and he had a deep scar running the length of one leg. As the bird cocked his head in Charlie's direction, he could see that it had lost an eye.

Charlie now felt a sudden warmth of affection for that bird he had seen only once, so long ago. He could see it as clearly as though it had happened that very morning. The bird had watched Charlie for a long time through its one eye, then bobbed its head up and down as though he were saying, "Yes" to him. At that moment, Charlie felt like a baby resting in God's arms – totally helpless on his own, yet absolutely protected from every possible danger. The last thing he remembered before falling asleep was hearing his guardian eagle squawking loudly and flapping his wings, as though broadcasting a warning to the world that Charlie was not to be disturbed.

Charlie never did know for sure whether that eagle came to him in the world of physical reality or in the world of dreams. He was never certain that the tattered feather he found in the rocks had come from this guardian eagle, or by some coincidence had been sitting there all along. It really didn't matter. From that moment forward, Charlie knew with absolute certainty that he would not be allowed to fail in his mission. He would have struggles, would have his feathers battered or might even lose an eye, but as long as he did not quit, he would prevail. In the years since, whenever it seemed that he was losing the battle, Charlie recalled that eagle who, if anything, was made even more majestic by his scars, and resolved to fight on.

My scars may not be as visible as the eagle's were, Charlie thought, but they are every bit as real. And now, my role in life will be to serve for Brian and the others in the way that eagle has served me – as a distant guardian. Charlie looked again at the four items on the desk. Then he laughed. Of all people, Brian Hunter did not need a motivational speech when he occupied this office. The two men would simply make small talk, and reminisce for a while. Then Charlie would leave. On his way out the door he would repeat the words that had guided him for so long:

DREAM A BIG DREAM,
MAKE IT A MEMORY OF
THE FUTURE,
AND EXPECT A MIRACLE.

EPILOG

# Dream Beyond the Dream

The morning chill had long since evaporated, so Charlie had tied his flannel hiking shirt to the outside of his backpack to let it dry. Almost exactly thirty years ago, he had written down in his *Dreamcyclopedia* a goal to spend a week alone hiking in the Grand Canyon. He'd never thought it would take this long, but now here he was, high on a ledge overlooking the Colorado River. He had not seen another human being in four days.

It was hard to maintain the appropriate state of awe in this magnificent cathedral, where every vista seemed to outdo the one before. As he rounded a corner, Charlie saw a hollow in the limestone wall that just seemed to cry out for him to stop and take a break. Dropping his backpack onto the ground, he extracted a bag of gorp, his water bottle, and his journal. He picked up his walking stick and turned it slowly in his hands, again reading each of the names that had been meticulously carved into it.

Each name brought back a memory of someone who had helped him build The Courage Place into a worldwide phenomenon – more a movement than a business – through which thousands of people had found a sense of direction, and the courage and determination to follow it. The business had grown in many directions that Charlie would never have anticipated in the early days, and the dream continued to get bigger and bigger.

The walking stick had been a gift at his retirement party several months earlier. It was presented to him by Cheryl von Noyes, who had become CEO of Future Perfect Now upon the retirement of Bill Douglas. "Just as we have leaned on you throughout the years," she'd said in her remarks, "now we want you to know that you can lean on us wherever your trail leads you." Charlie knew that was why he was in the Grand Canyon at this time, and why the trip had been delayed for so long. Thirty years ago, Alan Silvermane had told him to "Dream Beyond the Dream." Charlie hoped that Silvermane would have been proud of what he'd accomplished; the thirty-five year old Charlie who'd sat in the office with Silvermane would certainly been astounded to review the accomplishments of the sixty-five year old man he would someday become.

Although not many people knew the name Charlie McKeever, The Courage Place had become one of the world's most familiar brands. There was a Courage Place in almost every hospital, every airport, every shopping center, everywhere in the world. Every day, millions of people across the globe logged onto The Courage Place web site for a daily dose of education and inspiration. Courage Place graduates had started businesses which created millions of new jobs; served in local, state, and federal government at all levels; had started non-profit organizations and social service agencies to deal with the world's most pressing problems; and to Charlie most important of all, had become teachers, instructing the next generation on the skills and attitudes of courage and perseverance.

Now the time had come for Charlie to dream beyond the dream. He had plenty of money and, he hoped, a lot more time to continue making a difference, to continue creating an enduring legacy. For some time, he had been writing down ideas in his journal. He'd whittled that list down to a few that really excited him. In the next few days, he would decide upon one of them. Charlie opened the journal and reviewed his list again. It would be a tough choice. Looking down the river, he saw a tiny spot slowly growing larger as it came closer. It was unusual, he thought, to see a raven so high, flying solo, kiting the wind along the river. As it came closer, it squawked loudly, and Charlie realized that this was not a raven.

It was an eagle. It coasted down the river, like an angel dancing on the breath of God, closer to Charlie. When it was not twenty yards away, the eagle tilted on one wing and flew by so close that Charlie almost could have reached out and touched it with his walking stick. Now right above Charlie, the eagle flew down and squawked once more. Charlie looked up and looked into the face of his guardian eagle. He had only one eye.

Charlie closed his eyes and closed his journal, and smiled into the sun. He would sleep for awhile. And dream. A new dream. A big dream. The dream beyond the dream.

# THE END

# Spark Your Success – 8 unique audio CDs for building your business – and for building a great life

*Spark Your Success* features 8 full-length audio CDs that will revo-lutionize the way you see yourself, galvanize you to change your attitudes and behaviors, and catalyze you to take the immediate and sustained action to help you transform your dreams into memories of the future.

### CD #1: Get that Pickle Out of Your Mouth

How to have a more positive attitude and promote a more positive workplace.

### CD #2: 12 Steps to Manage Anxiety

How to transform the paralyzing negativity of fear into catalyzing energy for action.

### CD #3: Winning the War with Yourself

Using principles of military strategy to conquer YOWE (Your Own Worst Enemy).

### CD #4: Actions You Can Take to Have More Energy

Energy is life, and this CD will show you how to have more of it.

### CD #5: The Self-Empowerment Pledge

Seven Simple Promises that Will Change Your Life.

**CD #6: Building on the Pyramid of Self-Belief**

The four levels of self-belief, and how you can use them to build a better future.

**CD #7: The Magic of Metaphorical Visualization**

Revolutionary techniques to dream bigger dreams and make them real.

**CD #8: The Janitor in Your Attic**

An amazing motivational journey through your body to Spark you for Success, every day!

**Order this and other great products at**

**www.SparkStore.com**

**or call Values Coach at**

**800-644-3889 (319-624-3889)**

# SPARK PLUG PLUS

Spark Plug PLUS is a group coaching service focused on helping members achieve their goals by more effectively living their values. Our core curriculum is the 60-module course on *The Twelve Core Action Values*. This is complemented with a growing pool of other great resources. More than that, SP+ membership is a commitment that you make to yourself – and to the people who are important to you – that you will make the effort to assure that these twelve values, and the 48 cornerstones that put action into the values, are reflected in how you see the world, and in how the world sees you.

I know from having heard from hundreds of other Spark Plug PLUS members that you will consider this to have been one of the most effective, and cost-effective, investments you've made in yourself, your family, your career and your future.

When you join Spark Plug PLUS you will receive the 420-page workbook on *The Twelve Core Action Values*, which is filled with wisdom and ideas, strategies and exercises, and more than 500 excerpts from the books that could change your life (if you only had the time to read them). You will also have access to the SP+ members-only resource website, which features more than a hundred audio programs, e-books, and special reports. This includes the 12-CD audio album *True Wealth: Your Values and Your Money* which alone is worth more than the cost of membership. **These resources are only available to Spark Plug PLUS members and participants in Values Coach corporate training programs.**

**For more information or to join Spark Plug PLUS, call 800-644-3889 (319-624-3889). Tell them that you learned about it in *Your Dreams Are Too Small* and you will receive a discounted annual membership dues of only $56 (retail $98).**

# Have Joe Tye Share the Spark with Your Group

Joe Tye is CEO and Head Coach of Values Coach Inc., a company he founded in 1994. He is a dynamic, passionate and knowledgeable speaker who also knows that it takes "more than a pep rally" to change people's lives. He provides powerful and proven tools and techniques – like those featured in Your Dreams Are Too Small – and then inspires people to put them to work in their businesses and in their lives. Here's just some of what you can expect from a keynote by Joe:

- Practical skills for courage and perseverance based on the ultimate success formula: *Never Fear, Never Quit*
- The power of words, questions, and stories to supercharge your business and transform your life
- How to stop cheating yourself by settling for anemic dreams and goals, and practical strategies for thinking big, dreaming big, and achieving big
- Ten strategies to cultivate a more positive attitude and foster a more productive team environment
- The Power of Values to build a culture of ownership and a commitment to excellence

Joe is author of eleven books, including *Staying on Top When the World's Upside Down*, *Personal Best*, and the international bestseller *Never Fear, Never Quit: A Story of Courage and Perseverance.* His new book, *All Hands on Deck: Essential Lessons for Building a Culture of Ownership — From Legendary Business Leaders Who Did*, will be published by Wiley in July 2010. He will challenge, he will inform and teach, and he will inspire and motivate you to dream big dreams and achieve big goals. He is the ideal opening or closing keynoter for your program – and will give your audience a toolbox of take-home resources, *because it takes more than a pep rally to spark a business and to transform a life*!

## Typical testimonials from participants in one of Joe's programs

*"Probably the best, most inspirational program I've ever attended."*

–Sue Biskup, Owner of Brighton Insurance and Financial Services

*"Excellent program! Participants from our office gained some very valuable insights which we will be sharing with the rest of our staff. Not the usual hype and smoke. You gave us concepts that we actually can put to very good use in our agency."*

–Jim Elder, Elder Agency, Inc.

**For information about booking Joe as a speaker, call the Values Coach office at 800-644-3889 (319-624-3889) or contact Joe directly at joe@joetye.com**

# ACKNOWLEDGMENTS

Ten years ago, Jerry Jenkins and the crew at The Jenkins Group made the first edition of this book possible, and they have my lasting appreciation. The late Charlie Tremendous Jones and his team at Executive Books have been tremendous supporters. Katherine Glover was the spark plug who ignited this new edition, and has become a valued partner in helping us help others to dream bigger dreams.

The team in the Values Coach office keeps me busy, on track, and (usually) out of trouble – and they make work fun. Paula Yrigoyen, Michelle Arduser, Dick Schwab, the Dynamic Duo of Hung Viet Tran and Tung Hoang, and Miss Bonkers truly are my Dream Team.

It's been my privilege to work with some truly wonderful companies as Values Coach clients. In particular, Auto-Owners Insurance Company reflects the values, vision, and drive that are essential to making big dreams real. The opportunity to speak with the independent insurance agents who represent Auto-Owners has greatly influenced my own thinking about the secrets of success and achievement. I am forever grateful for meeting former Chairman and CEO Roger Looyenga the day my audience was making so much noise it interrupted his business meeting in the next room and he ended up inviting me to spend a day with the Auto-Owners executive team in Lansing, Michigan.

It's also been my privilege to work with a number of excellent speakers bureaus and meeting planners, all of whom I wish I could acknowledge in person. I've also been encouraged along the way by many other speaking professionals. In particular, I'd like to acknowledge Bob Burg (author of *Endless Referrals* and co-author of The *Go-Giver*), who was one of the earliest supporters of *Your Dreams Are Too Small.*

This is the third book I've worked on with Lisa Peterson, Michael Meister and their crew at Studio 6 Sense in Merrimac, Wisconsin, but I know it won't be the last.

Last but certainly not least, my eternal love and appreciation goes to my family. As daughter Annie and son Doug pursue their own dreams, they are a constant source of inspiration and frequent astonishment to their old man. Thirty-one years ago, I (literally) ran into the girl of my dreams. Today we have a fridge magnet in our kitchen that says "happiness is being married to your best friend." Sally is still the girl of my dreams, and I'm blessed to be married to my best friend.